RAISING
STRESS-PROOF
KIDS

Shelley Davidow is a teacher, author and trained facilitator in Restorative Practice. She has taught students aged from five to eighty and runs workshops nationally and internationally on the impact and management of stress at home, in the workplace and in the classroom. With her focus on social and emotional health, she has worked in schools across the US and Australia, conducting readings and workshops and facilitating discussions with young people on the many issues they confront. An award-winning author of over thirty-five books for children, teens and adults, her work deals with a wide range of social issues and is used in schools all over the world.

Praise for *Raising Stress-Proof Kids*:

'*Raising Stress-Proof Kids* provides eye-opening insight into how the unhealthy and unnecessary stresses of our educational systems, as well as outdated perspectives on parenting, are affecting our children.

It offers practical advice on how we can significantly and positively impact the lives of our children as they move through developmental phases and become mature, self-regulated and composed beings ready to succeed in our increasingly complex world.'

— ROLLIN MCCRATY PHD, INSTITUTE OF HEARTMATH, CALIFORNIA

RAISING STRESS-PROOF KIDS

Parenting Today's Children for Tomorrow's World

SHELLEY DAVIDOW MSEd

EXISLE
PUBLISHING

First published 2014

Exisle Publishing Pty Ltd
'Moonrising', Narone Creek Road, Wollombi, NSW 2325, Australia
P.O. Box 60–490, Titirangi, Auckland 0642, New Zealand
www.exislepublishing.com

A CiP record for this book is available from the National Library
of Australia

ISBN 978 1 921966 40 8

Design and typesetting by Big Cat Design
Illustration on page 44 courtesy of the Institute of HeartMath
Illustrations on pages vi–vii, 9, 25 and 153 courtesy of Shutterstock
Typeset in Minion Pro Regular 11.45 on 17.5pt
Printed in Shenzhen, China, by Ink Asia

This book uses paper sourced under ISO 14001 guidelines from
well-managed forests and other controlled sources.

10 9 8 7 6 5 4 3 2 1

Disclaimer
While this book is intended as a general information resource and
all care has been taken in compiling the contents, this book does not
take account of individual circumstances and is not a substitute for
professional advice. Neither the author nor the publisher and their
distributors can be held responsible for any loss, claim or action that
may arise from reliance on the information contained in this book.

Contents

Introduction *1*

PART ONE: STRESS

Stress Explained *10*

The Learned Stress Response *15*

The Heart–Brain Connection *17*

Positive Emotions and Stress *20*

PART TWO: ENVIRONMENTS

Out of the Womb: Babies and Toddlers *26*

Starting to Explore: Early Childhood *42*

Off to School: Ages Six and Up *56*

Emerging Adults: The Teenage Years *70*

The Academic Pressure Cooker *91*

The Physical Environment *97*

Virtual Reality *107*

Supportive Emotional Environments *119*

Finding the Right Educational Environment *133*

Stopping Stress in its Tracks *144*

PART THREE: **RESTORATIVE PARENTING**

Parenting for a Low-Stress Home   *154*

The Parent Toolbox   *166*

A Baby's Cry   *170*

Temper Tantrums   *172*

Sibling Rivalries   *183*

Friends and Enemies on the Playground   *189*

Dealing with Bullies   *193*

Independent Teens   *198*

Final Thoughts   *212*

Acknowledgements   214

Notes   215

Additional References   221

Index   223

INTRODUCTION

'What we are teaches the child far more than what we say, so we must be what we want our children to become.'
— Joseph Chilton Pearce, *Teaching Children to Love*

Here's a stressful thought: an estimated 16.7 million people worldwide die every year as a result of cardiovascular disease.[1] That's a staggering 43,835 people every single day who were children just a few decades ago. Heart disease kills more people in the developed world than any other cause, and we know that this tragedy doesn't happen overnight. Slowly, over time, hearts become diseased.

If that thought isn't enough to elevate blood pressure, here's another nerve-racking fact: stress (emotional and psychological) affects our hearts and nervous systems in complex and far-reaching ways. And it starts when we're young. Sometimes it begins before we're even born. It's part of our lives and it's often invisible.

Stress is rising alarmingly in our children, both at school and at home. Across the world, hearts are racing, faces are pale — and most of the time we're unaware that many of our children are chronically stressed. Teen suicide as a result of stress is on the rise and premature adult death as a result of the rising incidence of heart disease is climbing to greater heights every year. Stress, according to research done at VU University in the Netherlands, increases a person's risk of death five-fold.[2]

The link between stress and heart disease is a well-studied one, and an obvious one in certain respects, since stress negatively impacts our cardiovascular system by making our hearts race and flooding our systems with stress hormones. This is bad news for our health in the long term.

In 2006, a study at University College, London, involving more than 10,000 civil servants, found that adults with chronic work stress had double the odds of developing metabolic syndrome, a leading factor in diabetes and heart disease, than adults who weren't stressed. This was after controlling for other elements. Significantly, lead researcher Tarani Chandola said: 'The study provides evidence for the biological plausibility of psycho-social stress mechanisms linking stressors from everyday life with heart disease.'[3]

As the parents of today's children, we hold the future of *billions* of adults in our hands. Preventing our children from the long-term effects of stress is essential for their health and survival. But prevention has to begin early. We're a society with vast amounts of information at our fingertips and yet somehow we have to move from being a population that is well informed to a population that *acts* on that information, preventatively, if we want our children's generation to outlive ours.

Here's a thought to counter those preceding images of a world stressed to death: our children are not compelled to follow in our footsteps. The effects of stress, although pervasive, are eminently and, I believe, absolutely preventable.

This book is about and for all our children — our babies, our toddlers, our seven-year-olds, our teens — and the adults they will become. It's time we did something about the stresses our children are facing and the inadvertent role we often play in causing it. Pushing our children towards excellence, reacting stressfully to their behaviour and fearing for their futures often precipitates the very opposite outcome to the one we intend. The solutions are within our reach if we have the perseverance to make some radical changes in the ways in which we parent and educate.

As parents, we know, of course, that the children of today are the adults of tomorrow, and that the adults today who suffer the effects of a breathlessly fast-paced, competitive and stressful lifestyle with all its ensuing health issues were yesterday's children. When we hold our new-born babies in our arms, our most intense desire is to protect and care for them. We wouldn't dream of letting them go cold or hungry, nor could we stand to cause them pain or stress. When they cry, we comfort them. The earliest days of life are vulnerable and, as a society, we mostly understand that.

And then our children grow. We move them out into the world and gradually we stop listening to what their emotions and bodies are often telling us. We grow deaf to their demands, forget about how their environments and the adults around them impact their wellbeing, and we allow them to be 'socialised' in what anyone would call a tough world. We believe at some intrinsic level that stress is an ordinary, even necessary part of living in the world. In fact, many of us have come to take for granted that the sooner our children learn to 'toughen up', the better their chances of survival will be in this harsh and unforgiving world. In fact, this is the biggest fallacy.

At some point, our children may begin to let us know — often in fairly dramatic ways — that they aren't happy; that somehow they are stressed, overwhelmed and unable to cope. Sometimes they aren't able to 'toughen up' the way we expect them to do. This manifests as behaviour disorders, eating disorders, self-harm, withdrawal, learning disabilities, depression, and all the social and academic problems we can so easily identify in our homes or in any single school classroom today. It's not news that the fast-paced world in which our children live is vastly different from the environment of the past. And the struggles our children face are new and difficult.

Stress at school seems to be a factor worthy of consideration when we look at what's happening to our children around the world. High-stakes testing is one acute example of a stressor in our children's lives that comes at a price.

Over the years, standardised testing in the UK and US have taught us all that these tests are not a measurement of true aptitude. Wales, in the UK, has recently, after many years of rigorous high-stakes testing, dropped all standardised testing on students younger than fourteen. It is urging the rest of the UK to do the same. Boston College Education Professor Andy Hargreaves believes that 'Americans would do well to pause and take note of developments in Wales.' Australia might do too. Scotland pioneered the way in 2003 when it did away with testing students younger than fourteen. The Scottish Education Minister Peter Peacock stated that the emphasis would now be on 'teaching rather than testing'.[4] There's a unique idea.

Despite significant examples of the failure of high-stakes testing in the UK and US to enhance the aptitude and academic ability of students, Australia has modelled its testing program on an outdated process and is starting to experience the unwelcome effects on students after less than a decade of standardised national testing. NAPLAN (National Assessment Program — Literacy and Numeracy) tests, standardised tests given to students in years 3, 5, 7 and 9, are having a negative impact on Australia's children. Renowned Australian parenting expert and teacher Maggie Dent explains how children become anxiety-ridden, depressed and even suicidal. Researchers, she states, have found that children experiencing test stress revert to behaviours that show deep trauma. Her inbox is full of letters from parents who report that 'children in Year 3 are returning to bed wetting, anxiety disorders, hair pulling and are suffering "night terrors".' She writes, 'Look at the number of books and sample test questions on the market aimed at parents of Year 3 students. I mean, we're stealing childhoods here. This is all disturbing the developmental needs of children. We're pressuring them.'[5]

The Whitlam Institute at the University of Western Sydney conducted a review of academic literature on NAPLAN tests and revealed that the tests were 'a source of significant stress for young people and their families'.[6] Additionally, findings indicate that teachers are stressed as they focus on test-related material and turn away from holistic approaches. Stress because of these tests is transferred to relationships between parents and teachers, and parents and students.

Add this to the fact that one-quarter of Australia's population suffers from anxiety-related disorders, and it's obvious that there is very little awareness of how our parental and educational decisions affect the physiological and emotional make-up of our children.[7]

In 2003, the US Social Health Index, conducted by Innovation in Social Policy/Fordham University, stated that the nation's social health had reached its lowest point in 25 years. Youngsters were experiencing the worst of this; they seemed to have less of a sense of community than ever before and were more pessimistic, depressed and isolated.

Australia and the US aren't the only places where youngsters appear to be struggling. Peter Foster wrote from Beijing in the *Sunday Telegraph*, UK, on 11 March 2011:

> **A scientific survey of 9 to 12-year-olds in eastern China found that more than 80 per cent worried 'a lot' about exams, two-thirds feared punishment by their teachers and almost three-quarters reported fearing physical punishment from their parents.**

In the UK, the GCSE exams, which the majority of sixteen-year-olds have to sit, result in an inordinate amount of stress. A peek inside the head of one teen who wrote on a Yahoo chat site gives a brief look at how stressful the situation is for many youngsters:

**How can I cope with school stress (GCSEs)?
... I work from 8.45 until I go to bed, which I find
really stressful. [Mum] said she's not happy with my
progress ... I feel so under pressure and I feel like
school has ruined my life. All I do is this work. Any
ideas on how to help?**

**When I talk to my Mum ... she badgers me on what to
do ... I know she wants me to do well but it's all just
too much.[8]**

Is this a cry for help? When is 'too much' really too much? When we
don't hear or don't listen, our youngsters may resort to the last escape
route they see as available to them. This is the ultimate harm they can do
to themselves, the final, pointless, yet avoidable tragedy. Youngsters face
many stresses in their lives — at home as well as at school. It's clear that
exam pressure is a contributing factor in the depression and desperation
many of them feel. Liz Smith wrote on the World Socialist Website:

**In the past month there have been a number of
reports of how the pressure of school exams is
having a terrible impact on the mental wellbeing of
teenagers, with GPs prescribing anti-depressants
such as Prozac and Seroxat to help young people
deal with stress.[9]**

According to the Centers for Disease Control and Prevention (CDC),
in countries where mortality data is available, suicide rates as the third
leading cause of death in the 15 to 34 age group, preceded by accidents
and homicide. And the American Academy of Pediatrics reports that,

according to one study, 90 per cent of suicidal teenagers believed their families did not understand them.

In 2007, UNESCO's Report Card 7, 'Child Poverty in Perspective', gave a comprehensive overview of child wellbeing in rich countries. UNESCO assessed the lives and wellbeing of children and adolescents in economically advanced countries according to several criteria: material wellbeing; health and safety; educational wellbeing; family and peer relationships; behaviours and risks, and subjective wellbeing. There was insufficient data on Australia in this study, but the UK ranked second last and the US came last out of 21 countries.[10]

All is not well with our children.

So, my question is, if children spend the majority of their waking time at home and at school, are we, as parents and educators in the developed world, stressing our children to death? In our never-ending quest to make sure our children have the necessary tools and qualifications to survive in a competitive and global economy, have we, at some level, lost the plot? Are our educational systems and parenting techniques sometimes the very cause of our worst fears: the undermining of our children's ability to cope?

Stress is neither a necessary nor advantageous experience for growing children. Over the long term, the impact of a stressed nervous system is profoundly damaging to physiology, emotional stability and cognitive function.

Over the past 100 years, our lives have been made easier than they've ever been. Unprecedented advances at every turn make us feel like we're getting faster and smarter at something-or-other, by the minute. And yet, if the biggest killer in our fabulously fast-paced First World countries is heart disease, it might be worth looking at the price our children could end up paying for this 24/7 existence.

My research with the Institute of HeartMath in California (IHM) has led me to believe that we can go a long way towards addressing this problem by knowing a few fundamental things about stress, about its actual effect on our physiology, emotions and cognitive abilities, but most importantly, how to take conscious and well-informed steps to stop it before it becomes a chronic and overwhelming factor in our children's lives.

There are choices we can make about home environments, about our own responses to our children, which could have extraordinarily significant effects on their physiology, emotions and cognitive abilities. There are also informed choices we can make about our children's school environments, which could potentially have a long-term impact on the health, happiness and success of the next generation. This is of vital importance. In order to make those choices, though, we have to be informed and have a very practical understanding of the consequences of our own behaviour and decisions.

This book is the result of many years of experience and research. I hope my findings and suggestions will enable more adults (parents, carers and teachers) to be actively involved in working to create a less stressed, more successful and healthy generation.

KEY POINTS

- Stress is bad for children.

- Stress is linked to heart disease.

- Stress inhibits cognitive function in the long term.

- We can make choices that actively prevent stress.

- Environments impact on children's development.

Part One

STRESS

STRESS EXPLAINED

First of all, everyone needs to know that *stress disrupts healthy physiological, emotional and cognitive function.* That means, in simple terms, that when we're stressed our bodies stop functioning properly. We don't feel good. We can't think properly.

As a precursor to subsequent chapters, some fundamental explanations about the stress response might be helpful, so bear with me as I attempt to provide the ordinary person's guide to the brilliance of the autonomic nervous system.

Stress does have its place. Our bodies are wisely designed and the stress response is no exception. I grew up in Africa and now live in Australia. Both places are home to some rather exotic and poisonous creatures. Australia's Brown Snake is one of the deadliest snakes in the world: its venom is seven times more toxic than a South African Cape Cobra. The venom travels through the lymphatic system and can halt respiration and cause death in a matter of minutes. Recently I almost stood on one on a pathway to a friend's house and, as it turned towards me, my heart rate went from 60 to 120 beats per minute in a matter of seconds. I like to believe I have a respectful and healthy appreciation for snakes and that I don't fear them, but deeper instincts were at work as all the blood drained from my face, my legs began to shake, and I leapt and ran faster than I've ever run before up the verandah steps, where I was finally able to breathe out and even laugh at my close encounter, my dramatic 'narrow' escape.

This fight-or-flight response is the responsibility of the autonomic nervous system, which is made up of the *sympathetic* nervous system (or fight-or-flight capacity) and the *parasympathetic* nervous system (responsible for slowing the heart rate). While the first acts as an accelerator, the second acts as a brake. When we're confronted with a threat, it's the role of the sympathetic nervous system to:

1. accelerate heartbeat

2. stimulate secretion of stress hormones

3. cause a shift of blood supply towards the limbs and away from the brain.

So, when confronted with what I would call a valid stressor, something that is an actual threat to my existence (in this case, a snake), my sympathetic nervous system goes into action. In the short term, this is very helpful: with all the blood flowing rapidly away from my brain and into my limbs, and as glucose is released into my system, I can run like lightning — and escape. When I finally do escape and note that the threat has slithered off into the bushes, I heave a sigh of relief. I've used up the glucose and my heart rate slows, because now the parasympathetic nervous system becomes active. It's responsible for:

1. slowing the heartbeat

2. stopping the secretion of stress hormones

3. helping bloodflow to be directed optimally towards the brain.

The trouble is that even though we make the distinction *mentally* between a poisonous snake and an upcoming exam, our bodies do not. The body has the same response, whether we're being chased by a wild animal or facing a school quiz. This process is explained in depth by neuroscientist Robert Sapolsky in *Why Zebras Don't Get Ulcers*, an exhilarating, highly entertaining and sobering tome on the long-term effects of stress. Sapolsky describes how our bodies have not yet learned to differentiate in their responses whether the stressor is physically threatening or emotionally scary. So, your seven-year-old fretting over a spelling test or a page of forgotten homework, or your teenager having a meltdown over an upcoming exam, may well be having a physiological experience akin to being chased by a furious hippo or a hungry croc. But, when, for example, I run away from my snake, I actually make *use* of all the stress hormones and glucose and blood pounding away from my head to my limbs. And when I know I'm finally safe, the parasympathetic nervous system is allowed to take over, shift the balance and slow everything down, giving my heart a good rest.

Here's the problem: the longer and more frequent the stress, the more debilitating the results are on the body, the heart and the brain. So, if I'm stressing about an exam or a quiz, my body is still flooded with stress hormones such as cortisol and pumping with adrenaline, my heart is still racing, just as if my life were actually in danger, but I'm not running anywhere and for weeks, maybe months at a time I'm not about to reach a place where I can 'breathe out' and let the parasympathetic nervous system kick into gear. And after a while, the body gets to a point when the sympathetic nervous system has trouble turning itself off. The brakes fail. The adrenals 'burn out'. Our brains, our limbs and, in particular, our hearts were not designed for sustained, long-term fight-or-flight.

Feeling chronically stressed these days usually has little to do with actual threats to our safety, unless we're living in a war zone or being faced with successive natural disasters. But the *perception* of threats to our safety acts on us in the same way as an actual threat.

We sit at home, or at work or school, 'stressing' about all kinds of things. As parents, we might be worried about finances, our children's behaviour, their social issues, a betraying spouse, an alimony payment that has not arrived. We're stressed about job security and burnout. Children are often overwhelmed with pressures to succeed socially or academically, with worries about peers, parents, relationships and test results. All this sets hearts racing, makes palms sweaty and ultimately diverts blood from our brains, making us pale, scatty and short-tempered.

We think that rushes of adrenaline make us feel good and sharpen our wits. In reality, however, adrenaline in excess is toxic. This is why we feel sick during a really frightening episode, regardless of whether we're running from a predator or fretting about an exam. Children who are significantly stressed about something will often complain of stomach aches and nausea. Stress makes us acutely sick and can lead to chronic disease.

The problem with our modern-day stresses and stressors is that there's no immediate set of steps to a safe verandah. We never really escape the deadly snakes of our own thought processes that are having the same physiological effect on us as if we were in a real, life-threatening emergency. Our parasympathetic nervous system doesn't get the chance to regain a balance.

Sometimes a glass of wine, or a nice cold beer, or harder substances, might seem to be the only escape from this invisible, many-headed animal we call 'stress'.

Obviously, this state of affairs can adversely impact our immune systems, our endocrine systems and our vital organs. The free advice that we've grown deaf to when we're stressed are the clichés that tell us to

1) breathe deeply 2) meditate or 3) do some yoga. It's advice that seems pathetic when we're feeling *really* on edge, when our fight-or-flight response is an out-of-control train plummeting down a steep track. And yet this advice is worthy of attention.

In light of our children's developing nervous systems, one of the most essential habits we can develop as parents is to modify our own stress response to situations. In the next chapter it will become clear why this is such a vital step on the long and winding parenting road.

KEY POINTS

- Stress disrupts healthy physiological function.

- The sympathetic nervous system turns stress hormones 'on' to escape danger.

- The parasympathetic nervous system turns stress hormones 'off' once danger has passed.

- Stress is only 'good' in the short term to enable us to escape a threat.

- In many respects, our bodies don't distinguish between real and perceived threats.

THE LEARNED
STRESS RESPONSE

You might be wondering why it is that some children take things lightly and cruise through the very same stressors that make others fall apart. The answer might lie as far back as a few generations: stress response is learned and carried on from one generation to the next in detailed and various ways. Sapolsky explains how stressed mothers 'teach' their babies while they are still in the womb to have an overactive stress response: 'Anxiety revolves around a part of the brain called the amygdala, and prenatal stress programs the amygdala into a lifelong profile that has anxiety written all over it.'[1]

A pregnant woman who is constantly stressed is flooding her body (and the body of her unborn baby) with stress hormones. As adrenaline and cortisol rush through her, they rush through her baby. Babies begin 'learning' about their surroundings while they're in the womb. The womb makes up their immediate environment and their bodies are adapting to it; they are already being conditioned to either have an overactive stress response, or not. And this stress response, once learned, is hard, though not impossible, to re-design.

I was a very stressed pregnant woman for several months. We were in South Africa. Moments of extreme stress happened when 1) twelve armed intruders made their way through our garden en-route from a robbery at the house behind us, and 2) more armed intruders broke into our home office to help themselves to electronic equipment, and 3) I was by then so terrified that dogs barking or twigs cracking outside became a herald of some danger and I awoke all through each night, heart pounding, my unborn baby awake and kicking as my stress became his.

My fight-or-flight mechanism was in overdrive. And that had effects for years on my child, who had been primed into having an over-active stress response by his mother. But even when a child is born with an over-active sympathetic nervous system, the immediate environments and the people in those environments as a child grows can have a profound impact on the developing brain and slowly maturing nervous system.

The impact of our behaviour as parents, on our children, can have a real effect. It's *this* impact and how to make it beneficial for our children and for their futures that is the subject of this book.

KEY POINTS

- Stress response is already being learned by babies in the womb.

- Even before birth, babies' nervous systems are affected by their mothers.

- The environment surrounding newborn babies affects their neurological development.

THE HEART–BRAIN
CONNECTION

Our society operates most often as if our heads and hearts (our minds and our feelings, or our thinking and our emotions) are separate entities, not just metaphorically but also physiologically. The cliché is that the one is always doing things at the expense of the other: if we follow our hearts, somehow it's implied that we aren't thinking too clearly. If we follow our heads, well, then we're being cold rationalists. It's probably time to let go of these old paradigms and start seeing things in perspective — and there's nothing like a bit of scientific evidence to help us along the way.

Since 1991, the Institute of HeartMath in California (IHM) has been doing research on the heart–brain connection and measuring physiological responses to different emotional states. According to the IHM, our hearts have an innate 'intelligence'. Hearts respond to the environment, and the people in that environment, every second of the day. They are either racing with fear or pounding with love or excitement. We get a 'sense' of our emotional states from our hearts.

So, instead of the heart being viewed as a glorified pump, we might start looking at it as a sense organ. It lies at the centre of our rhythmic systems and generates a large, measurable, electromagnetic field. Oxytocin (the love or bonding hormone) is secreted by the pituitary gland, at the base of the brain. But, surprisingly, oxytocin levels within the heart have been measured and findings published by the IHM show levels in the heart as high as those found in the brain.[2] So, when we feel love, it's perhaps not surprising that we experience the emotion in the region of our hearts, rather than in our knees or our kidneys!

That old division, the one between the head and the heart or our thoughts and our feelings, might well be reassessed in the light of new research:

> **The latest research in neuroscience confirms that emotion and cognition can best be thought of as separate but interacting functions or systems, each with its unique intelligence … [R]esearch is showing that the key to the successful integration of the mind and emotions lies in increasing the coherence (ordered, harmonious function) in both systems and bringing them into phase with one another.[3]**

So, if we're feeling love and gratitude, we're having an impact on our cognitive function, on how we think. Likewise, if I'm stressed as I think I'm being pursued up the garden path by a deadly Antipodean viper, and my heart is racing with fear, my brain is being impacted in a measurable way.

Neurocardiology is a relatively new field. According to Professor Rollin McCraty and his team of researchers at the IHM, messages going from the heart to the brain are twice as frequent as messages going the other way.[4] That's something worthy of a few moments' consideration.

Every emotion our children experience throughout the day, *everything they feel* from the moment they are born, has a direct effect on the function of their autonomic nervous systems *and* their brains. This idea might challenge many preconceived notions of 'the way things are'.

What children *feel* as a result of the people and environments to which they're exposed on a daily basis can be a vitally important part of what forms their cognitive or intellectual make-up, their emotional responses and, consequently, their behaviour. This is potentially all written into neural circuitry, into the way an individual responds to the world.

KEY POINTS

- The heart is not a glorified pump.

- Emotion and cognition are separate but connected functions.

- Ordered, harmonious emotions can lead to ordered, harmonious cognitive functions.

- Feeling love and gratitude positively impacts cognitive function.

- What children feel throughout the day is written into neural circuitry.

POSITIVE EMOTIONS AND STRESS

The function of the autonomic nervous system, the human stress response and the role of the heart and how it relates to parenting will hopefully all become clear in this chapter. And this knowledge can then form the fundamental basis for every parenting decision. It certainly became the life raft that I climbed onto on this sometimes wild and terrifying parenting ride. It's knowledge that has stood me in good stead whether I was responding to minor issues or major meltdowns.

And so, a bit more science …

Heart rate variability (HRV) is the beat-to-beat variation of the heart. Our hearts are at the centre of our 'rhythmic systems'. They're not metronomes with a steady rhythm of 65 or 70 beats a minute. A *high* degree of variability is a good thing. It's predictive of emotional and cognitive adaptability and openness. A *low* degree is often predictive of emotional disturbances and behaviour disorders.

Here's an experiment. Take a deep breath in and, as you do so, take your pulse. Then, keeping your finger on your pulse, breathe out slowly. If you're sensitive, you might notice that when you breathe in, your heart beats slightly faster. When you breathe out, it slows down. That's because when you breathe in, the sympathetic nervous system is activated and accelerates your heart rate. Breathe out, and the parasympathetic nervous system comes into action and slows it down. Very simply put, the sympathetic nervous system signals 'Go!' and the parasympathetic system signals 'Whoa!' That's a bit of an oversimplification, but you get the picture.

Ever catch yourself sighing with exasperation or frustration? We sigh when things are too much, when we're stressed, when our bodies know intrinsically that they need to slow down. Our bodies have an innate wisdom and sometimes, such as when we sigh, we're activating the parasympathetic nervous system so that we don't go into overdrive.

Our heart rates vary throughout the minute and throughout the day, depending on what we're thinking, feeling and experiencing.

> **HRV patterns are extremely responsive to emotions, and *heart rhythms tend to become more ordered, or coherent, during positive emotional states* [emphasis added].**[5]

Regardless of age, therefore, HRV patterns will vary depending on our emotional states. And just as stress affects our bodies adversely over the long term, so positive emotional states can have a far-reaching impact on our bodies and our minds, not just in the moment but also over time.

A balanced autonomic nervous system is a wonderful thing. It means we avoid overdrive, we don't burn out, and our bodies can age and do a substantial amount of mileage without breaking down. It's a fact: our physiology is constantly responding to our thoughts and feelings. What happens in our *hearts* influences our *brains'* electrical activity. In terms of our children's wellbeing, in terms of their emotional and academic success in the world as they grow, this is crucial.

When someone's in a positive emotional state, something fairly dramatic happens. It's just as dramatic as 'fight or flight', but at the relaxing, happy end of the spectrum. A baby being held in a loving embrace and soothed by a familiar, loving voice is experiencing a positive emotional state. In this state, heart rhythms become more ordered. This, in turn, affects the growing brain's electrical activity. It's quite a responsibility to think that much of our children's neural patterning is being set up before they're capable of remembering the experiences that are forming those patterns.[6] The term 'high coherence', as determined by the IHM, refers to a physiological state. It's defined as follows:

> **Psycho-physiological coherence ... involves a high degree of balance, harmony and synchronization within and between cognitive, emotional and physiological processes. Research has shown that this state is associated with high performance, reduced stress, increased emotional stability and numerous health benefits.[7]**

From the smallest baby to the oldest adult, a sustained positive emotional state is going to have a marked effect on cognitive, emotional and physiological processes. And the tricky thing is, we can't fake a positive emotional state. It doesn't help to 'grin and bear it' or to 'smile and pretend to be happy'. We have to feel this state deeply, over an extended period of time.

When a person is in a state of high coherence physiologically, everything is functioning at optimum level. It's interesting though by no means surprising that the heart rhythm pattern of someone feeling frustration is jagged and uneven, while the pattern of someone experiencing an extended state of appreciation is a flowing sine wave. This indicates 'high coherence'.

Below is an example of each of these states:[8]

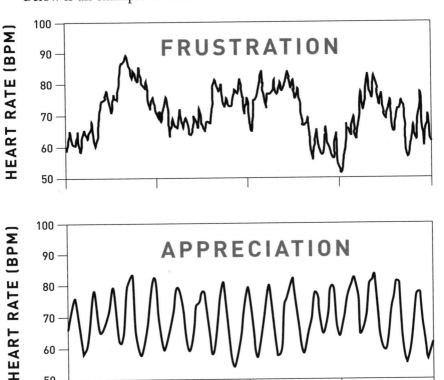

'There are organism states in which the regulation
of life processes becomes efficient, or even optimal,
free-flowing and easy. This is a well-established
physiological fact. It is not a hypothesis.'[9]

If we want to address the crisis our children are facing at home and
at school, across the world, it's in our interests and theirs to begin to
understand how the environment and the people in it impact them. As
parents, we can make decisions based on the knowledge that we need to
support an optimal state in our children, where all processes are efficient

and stress doesn't overwhelm them and put them at a disadvantage. Because stressed children *are* disadvantaged. Their bodies are affected. Their cognitive capacity is affected. An environment that is loving, supportive and coherent allows children to experience high coherence; and ordered harmonious heart rhythm patterns reflect in enhanced cognitive function. Feeling happy and loved and *un*stressed makes children smarter. Imagine that.

KEY POINTS

- What happens in our hearts influences the brain's electrical activity.

- 'High coherence' is an ordered, harmonious, psycho-physiological state.

- A sustained positive emotional state has a positive effect on cognitive function.

- We can't fake a positive emotional state.

- As parents, we can put our children at an advantage by providing a positive emotionally supportive environment.

Part Two

ENVIRONMENTS

OUT OF THE WOMB:
BABIES AND TODDLERS

Our most basic instinctive knowledge tells us that the miracle of life depends crucially on the environment that supports it.

Before we're born, our environment is of fundamental importance. It's obvious that a foetus needs the protection of the womb and the nutrients that come from the mother in order to survive. As intelligent adults we know this. A baby born at 26 weeks needs an extensive array of high-tech equipment to keep it alive as science does its utmost to recreate a womb equivalent. An incubator with tubes and pipes is hardly a substitute for the warm, watery environment from which the baby has just emerged, but it does enable babies to survive in many cases. Before 26 weeks, most babies cannot survive outside the womb. Little lungs in particular need the environment of the womb to develop fully, and so, even when these premmies survive, their lungs are often weak as a result of entering our oxygen–nitrogen-rich environment too early. It's obvious in this instance that an environment that is fine and healthy for a toddler is not good for a 26-week foetus. We can easily see that the environment at the beginning stage of human life is critically important — a matter of life and death, literally.

When women are pregnant, they worry about what they eat and drink, they exercise and care for their bodies perhaps more than at any other time in their lives. But they might not be so aware that what they think and, most significantly, what they *feel* will also form an integral part of a child's prenatal environment.

Stress a pregnant mother, flood her system with stress hormones on a chronic basis, and her baby may well carry this impact, this pattern of an over-active stress response, throughout their life. So, even though the womb is physically the perfect place for a growing foetus, the emotional state of the mother is another influential factor in the healthy physical, emotional and intellectual development of our unborn babies.

However, when our babies are born, it seems to me that we slowly start to lose sight of the fact that the environment plays a crucial role in how babies and children develop. It's easy to forget that each stage of development as a baby grows into an adult requires a different type of environment in order for that human being to be physiologically, emotionally and intellectually sound.

Certainly, what's essential for one phase is no longer necessary for the next. Stress often happens when we forget that these phases are *real* — they're tied to our children's physiological, emotional and cognitive development — and we often hurry our children into an environment for which they're underprepared. Children are not miniature adults. A toddler is not a small teen. Each phase is distinctive and our children grow slowly from one into the next.

It's worth remembering that doing what's right for our children is all about timing. The right 'thing' at the right time makes all the difference: helping a nine-month-old into a standing position is absolutely fine, but we'd never do that to a three-month-old for fear of damaging the child's body; we know that such a small skeleton is soft; we know that the muscles aren't sufficiently developed. It takes years for bones and joints to mature. In the same way, teaching three-year-olds to read before their neural networks are sheathed with myelin is counter-productive. It takes a full 25 years for a brain to reach maturity. We don't expect toddlers to learn to drive cars, but we do expect sixteen-year-olds to do just that. Developmentally they're ready. My point is that when our babies are small, we're quite good at recognising what they can and cannot do. As they grow into toddlers and children, however, we lose sight of the fact that each new stage in their development comes with new capacities, and we should be mindful of this so that we don't cause stress and damage by imposing expectations on them that are ahead of where they're at.

Of course, children do develop at slightly different rates from one another, so what's right for one four-year-old may not yet be quite right for another five-year-old. It really is up to us as parents to make careful individual decisions as we observe the unique process of a particular child's development. In general, though, there are solid physiological markers that we could look at to divide childhood into distinct phases. We'll look at these in more detail later.

There really is a time for everything — even a time to rebel and argue with the parents who have loved you so selflessly all your life! If the time is wrong, our children usually let us know. But we have to be listening in the right way. With our hearts. Literally.

It takes a baby a full nine months to be ready for the world. Nine months before a child can breathe air — that's quite a long time! And then, when our children are born, they don't immediately see properly. Their skins are delicate. Their bodies are uncoordinated. It makes sense then that we put our tiny babies in an environment that closely resembles the one they've just left. Soft colours, low lighting and soft textures on their skin will enable them to slowly open their eyes and begin to make sense of the world around them. I've seen a few newborn babies inside malls and shopping centres, where loud noise and flickering fluorescent lights have overwhelmed them. The sensory overload for a newborn is very possibly the equivalent of being pushed into an icy pool; it's a stressful and physically shocking experience for which the body isn't yet prepared.

And yet, in this shopping scenario, perhaps the mother has no choice — shopping must be done and this is the only time. But she might be able to carry her newborn in a sling close to her, and even throw a piece of pink silk over her shoulder and the baby's head, so that the baby is protected from the harsh world while it is still so sensitive.

In these early days and weeks and months, when my son was a tiny delicate six-pounder, I received lots of free 'expert' advice. Firstly, said my friends, he needs to learn independence. Put him in his crib in his own room and let him cry. You'll soon be sleeping through the night. Well, at first I wondered why their words unsettled me, but it didn't take me too long to figure it out. We spend the best part of our 80 average years of life as independent human beings. A baby is by its very nature a dependent being. If that being depends entirely on me, for a few short weeks or months or years, I need to be part of an environment that is dependable. Those were my thoughts. My son had just spent nine full months inside my body, underneath my heart. The next logical step for his healthy development would be to have him next to me, on my skin and close to me, so that the transition into this next phase of his life would be a smooth one without undue stress. The environment would need to be a small step away from the one he'd just left, and would include, most importantly, my physical presence.

What babies need as the most pervasive element in their immediate environment is love. Leaving them to cry when they need us is a trauma. When we don't respond, we teach them that their most fundamental need for comfort and touch and love is not going to be met. And the reason 'controlled crying' and other such techniques often leave parents feeling as though they have broken their babies' hearts is because they have. The stress experienced by babies who are left to cry is written into their neural patterning.

A 2012 study by Wendy Middlemiss from the University of North Texas measured the levels of cortisol, the stress hormone, in babies who were left to 'cry it out', or 'self-soothe', to get themselves to sleep during the night. The study found that although the babies did eventually stop the physical behaviour of crying, over the course of three nights, they still exhibited elevated cortisol levels when they woke or transitioned from waking to sleeping.[1] Middlemiss writes: 'Although the infants exhibited no behavioural cue that they were experiencing distress at the transition to sleep, they continued to experience high levels of physiological distress, as reflected in their cortisol scores. Overall, outward displays of internal stress were extinguished by sleep training. However, given the continued presence of distress, infants were not learning how to internally manage their experiences of stress and discomfort.'[2]

So, Middlemiss's research finally supports those parents who think that letting babies cry themselves to sleep is potentially harmful. We create stress by withholding our love and comfort from our children when they are most vulnerable.

Tanya had her baby while we were still in our early twenties and was determined that her life wouldn't change after the birth of her son. He wasn't going to stop her from doing her thing, which included going to parties where loud music almost shattered my eardrums and spending time with her childless friends. She said he'd get used to it — the sooner the better.

But a baby's ears are far more sensitive than an adult's. They have a much wider hearing range. Babies hear things that we don't. Tanya grew annoyed that her baby cried so much, though he would always eventually go to sleep. He slept restlessly, half-waking with a jolt with every new and different beat of each new song. He did learn to cope. As human beings, we do learn to survive. But his nervous system was tweaked and his sensitive ears were bombarded with loud noise for which his baby sense of hearing was not yet designed. The pragmatist in me would say that a late-night party with heavy loud music is not an ideal environment for a developing foetus or a young child and seems hardly the kind of place where a baby can develop optimum physiological, emotional and intellectual capacities. The researcher in me understands that noise is both *heard* by a foetus and *felt* as vibrations. It's transmitted though amniotic fluid and bones. Loud noises can impact foetal and child development in fairly negative ways. For an unborn baby exposed to excessive noise, cochlear development can be impaired, which can result in hearing loss. Also, unborn babies and young children cannot control the environment or take themselves away from the noise. And, because they haven't developed adequate coping mechanisms during this critical period in relation to learning, psychological as well as physiological damage can follow.

In fact, exposure to too much noise in utero can result in lifelong impairment of learning and education; it can manifest as a short-term deficit followed by adaptation as these tiny human beings learn to cope, but the disadvantages are enormous.[3] So, it's worth waiting until our babies are old enough to be left at home with a loving babysitter, before we head out to the next rock concert.

My son let us know very early on that loud noises were not for him. When the phone rang, he was always startled and cried; the vacuum cleaner upset him; a friend who had a persistent cough terrified him. We were at a loss for what to do with our overly sensitive baby who could not seem to cope with noise. Our well-meaning friends told us it was time to desensitise him, toughen him up. My first response was, okay, let's try this — life will be a lot easier and we can have Adam, our coughing friend, round without him feeling holy terror every time he has to cough. But then I thought, why? It would really only be for our convenience. Why put our tiny baby through the torture of exposing him over and over again to something with which he obviously could not yet cope?

I had an innate sense that exposing him to noise that upset him was counter-productive. I also guessed that he wouldn't still be crying when the phone rang when he was one or three or thirteen years old. So, we didn't desensitise him. We turned the ringer off all the house phones except for the one furthest from his room, so that the ring was a distant, non-alarming sound; one of us took our son for a walk while the other vacuumed. Housework definitely took longer than it might have. And we stopped fretting about our coughing friend, figuring that this human sound was not as violent or shocking as the other two. He got over his sensitivity to loud noises, although even at three, when the vacuum cleaner went on, he took himself outside to play.

When he was about nine we discovered he had just about perfect pitch. He's now a gifted teenage classical musician who plays the double bass and the organ. He's still sensitive to sound but in a very different way. Recently he had the chance to practise Bach at St Peter Mancroft Church in Norwich, England. The sound was so loud and so enormous that it reverberated through my whole body — and I was far away from the pipes, standing on the gravestone of some poor soul from the 1300s. Everything shook, even the stones beneath my feet vibrated as he pulled out more stops for the final chords of a well-known fugue. I can't imagine what might have been the result had I attempted to 'desensitise' him.

The environment in which our small children grow is certainly comprised of the places they spend most of their time, but most importantly, the early environment is made up of the family and friends who surround them.

Of course, we know that there has to be a degree of physical stability or our children won't survive. We usually clothe them properly in cold weather and dress them lightly in warm weather. I have, though, witnessed a young mother in the UK dressed warmly on a cold winter's day, carrying her baby who had no hat, gloves or wrappings, and whose tiny legs were jutting out of his little suit, almost purple with cold; and in Australia a mother left her baby in a pram, overdressed in stifling heat, while she went for a swim in the sea! But let's hope these are the exceptions and that for the most part we're pretty good at taking care of our babies' obvious physical needs.

One of the most important aspects that we often don't consciously consider, as we would the weather or hunger and thirst, is the emotional environment that surrounds our babies. It's just as important, if not more so, than the physical one.

Firstly, it makes a significant difference whether we are held to our mother's hearts after we're born or left in a crib in a poverty-stricken orphanage. Thanks to the controversial (and inordinately cruel) experiments on baby rhesus monkeys by Harry Harlow in the 1950s, we can now say with certainty that loving touch is the most basic and essential element that a baby needs from its mother — over and above food and protection. Harlow separated baby monkeys from their mothers and gave them two surrogates. One was a terry-cloth substitute with a rudimentary face. The other was a metal wire mesh version with a nipple that dispensed milk. The baby monkey attached itself to the cloth mother, and 'loved' it, spending on average far more time with the cloth mother than with the milk-producing wire mesh mother. Harlow wrote, 'The primary function of nursing … is that of insuring frequent and intimate body contact of the infant with the mother.'[4]

Your four-week-old who wants to nurse every two hours instead of every four wants you to hold him close more than he wants breast milk or formula.

If the little monkey's cloth mother was removed, the monkey

screamed and threw fits. Think of how many children have attached themselves to some old cloth or blanket and won't go anywhere without it. It is a soft surrogate that the child can touch and hold. Harlow's experiments proved what many people might say is obvious: if you isolate a baby from its mother, and deprive it of touch, you create complete stress and distress, with long-term consequences in terms of social, emotional and intellectual development.[5]

As a result of Harlow's work, loving touch is now part of many programs in neonatal intensive care units (NICUs), where babies range in age from 23 gestational weeks to 36. It's also used in orphanages, where it was once thought that providing food and shelter was enough to enable young children's survival. Loving touch is arguably the most vital element in healthy emotional, intellectual and physiological development. When our babies or young children are upset or distressed, we hug them and hold them close. Our physical proximity reduces stress and anxiety and comforts them.

I know that millions of mothers all over the world have to go back to work within weeks of giving birth. In developed countries, it's become accepted practice to place your three-month-old in day care. I would, though, suggest that because of rules and regulations and limited time, the amount of cuddling, hugging and touching that goes on in a day care centre is not always optimal and often nothing like what the baby would receive at home. Day care for babies and very small children might come at a cost that's higher than expected.

In the US state of Oregon, I visited a day care centre where my friend's child spent eight hours a day, four days a week, from three months old to three years, after which she moved on to preschool. The place was clean and full of bright happy colours and lots and lots of children, all engaged in either playing or being fed by a carer or eating. Nowhere, in the long half an hour I spent there, did I see any of the children being hugged or held, or lovingly stroked, just for the sake of it. Sure, they were picked up and changed or cleaned or moved, but that's a different kind of touch to loving, comforting cuddles. Studies in NICUs reveal that being touched procedurally, even for the tiniest premature babies, is a stressor rather than a comfort. As a result of this, NICU infants are now exposed to a certain amount of non-procedural touch in order to 'promote comfort', and minimise the stress that is so obviously part of the NICU environment. Research on the types of touch that promote comfort are underway.[6]

My concern is for millions of children who don't get the essential doses of cuddles and affection when they're very small. For a start, I have to say that the little girl who had spent her early life in that day care centre was a handful at home. She yelled, she bit, she grabbed things from other toddlers. She smacked them on the head when they came near her. She was tough. She knew how to survive. She was properly desensitised and 'socialised'. You could take her anywhere and leave her with anyone. But at what cost?

Of course, not every day care centre is the same and there are many environments where children are lovingly cared for and where lots of cuddles are dispensed.

My colleague Karen sent her daughter to a day care centre in New South Wales, Australia, where, she says, '[The centre] is technically billed as "long day care" covering kids aged 0 to 6. I can best sum it up as being an environment where you can absolutely "feel the love"!' Karen describes the centre as going to 'great pains to ensure continuity of staff members if people go on maternity leave, etc. Gillian [daughter] will have been there for three years and she'll only ever have had four main staff looking after her — although she knows (and hugs!) all the others.' Karen describes the place as offering 'huge amounts of affection on display all the time'. She notes how the staff sing and play with the children, getting into the sandpit with them or even rolling with them on the ground, as any involved parent would. The only thing that she and her partner are anxious about is how 'the tears will flow on both sides' when their daughter leaves at the end of the year.

Karen's daughter is a bright, compassionate and inquisitive child who feels safe in the world. So, it makes sense to me that if we have to leave our little ones with other people in an environment away from home, there are some careful choices that we can make to ensure our children get the essential nurturing they need.

Millie, who lives in Queensland, Australia, has just had her third child. She's a calm, sweet person, and though she and her husband have been struggling financially, she's taken time out from work to stay with her new baby. Whenever she goes out, her baby is attached to her in a sling, and he's as calm and peaceful as she is. He only cries when some-one takes him out of view of his mother. Being around him is like being with a little Buddha. He radiates tranquillity. He smiles at everyone. There's clearly not a lot of stress in his life. And it shows.

From birth to three, the prefrontal cortex is going through one of its most rapid development and pruning phases. Children at this young age have to learn that their hands and feet are attached to them, and then they have to gradually coordinate them. They have to make meaning out of the words they hear. They have to form words to make meaning. It's unprecedented how exponential learning is in these early years. If envi-ronment and the emotional state of a child is a critical factor in cogni-tive development, then the environment that surrounds our children in these early years is going to be as influential as the womb was when our children were there.

Of course, necessity sometimes makes it impossible for parents to take care of their babies full time. But I would say that there are environments that closely approximate home, and that if babies and toddlers do have to be cared for by someone else, it makes a great deal of sense to find a small day care centre, even a co-op run by friends, where babies can form a loving attachment to the adult who is with them for eight hours; an environment where children are hugged, held and touched by someone who loves them, and with whom they can develop a warm relationship.

Being deprived of a loving parent is an acute stressor for young children. We talk about 'separation anxiety' as if it's something abnormal, a kind of affliction that has to be cured. Sure, we've all had to leave our children crying at some point in our lives, but I think it makes a difference when that happens, and how.

Josh and Amanda were friends of mine who decided that their baby would go to bed at 6 p.m. from the time she was three weeks old and sleep through the night, on her own. They'd put her down in her crib and close the door. Then they'd turn up the TV so they couldn't hear her screaming. I was so stressed by their baby's distress that I stopped visiting them or stopping in at any time of day when their little girl might be going to sleep or going down for a nap. The child learned that when she cried in her crib she would not be attended to. We know enough now about elevated stress hormone levels to support the idea that letting children cry themselves to sleep is not the most beneficial approach.

I've seen later how these children are often the ones who try all kinds of other ways to get attention. Simply crying for help is not one of their options.

My son was my biggest teacher in this regard. He did not sleep for longer than two-hour stretches for the first three years of his life. My husband and I were convinced we were going to die of exhaustion. Letting our baby cry was far too distressing. We felt for him: he had eczema, he had colic, he needed us. We set up a separate bedroom for the person not on duty and took shifts throughout the night. While I was breastfeeding, I took the shift from bedtime to 3 or 4 a.m. My husband took the early morning shift. I learned that I could function okay if I got even just a three-hour stretch of unbroken sleep. When we finally slept our first seven-hour night, I woke up in the morning and realised I was back! I felt like I'd been in a twilight zone for years. I could love everyone and be genuinely civil to strangers again. At a recent dinner party with friends who have a baby, we were discussing sleep. I mentioned that we couldn't let our son cry himself to sleep. When I joked to my son, 'I don't know, maybe we should have just abandoned you to your own devices, even just for one night,' he wrapped his long teenage arms around both of us and said seriously, 'I'm glad you didn't.'

He's just become the youngest glider pilot in Australia. This, from a sensitive, shy little boy who apparently, according to my friends, needed to 'toughen up and learn how to socialise'. So, although he's too young to even get his learner's licence in a car in Australia, he can soar above the freeway at 3000 feet. His quiet sense of self-assurance and his integrity have earned him the respect of his flying instructors who commend his responsible attitude in the air. I'm aware that the way we loved and supported him through his extremely challenging early years was viewed as 'overprotective' by almost everyone around us … but the drawbacks were all ours and the benefits belong to him.

So, to those exhausted parents who fear having to sleep next to their children 'forever', here's a quick thought as you negotiate the right time for your child to have their own sleeping space: babyhood and early childhood, when your child physically needs you, is brief. Patting, comforting, reassuring your child as they get used to being away from you, is a gentle, less stressful approach. I trust that you won't still have your thirteen-year-old in your bed.

The philosophy I'm employing here is a kind of emotional pragmatism: what makes sense? For a tiny baby, it does make sense that they are close to their parents. But it's more than emotional pragmatism that we need when we consider our children's environments.

If we want to raise intelligent, well-adjusted children who will be bright and happy *and* healthy, we have to consider this fact: everything that goes on in a child's heart, from before birth onwards, also goes on in their head.

That's quite a concept. Our brains respond to our heart's rhythms. Our children's brainwaves entrain to their heart's rhythms. Harmonious ordered patterns in heart rhythms result in harmonious ordered patterns in their brains. That's profound. If you want to think clearly, calmly, logically — if you want an optimal cognitive state — your heart rhythms have to be coherent.

Here are two diagrams that show how a coherent heart rhythm pattern, generated when a person is sustaining a deep feeling of appreciation or gratitude, leads to the brainwaves becoming entrained with the heart. The picture below records a person's heart rhythms; the picture overleaf records their brainwave rhythms. The small diagrams on the left show how the heart and brain become synchronised, peaking and dipping at the same time.[7]

HEAD–HEART ENTRAINMENT

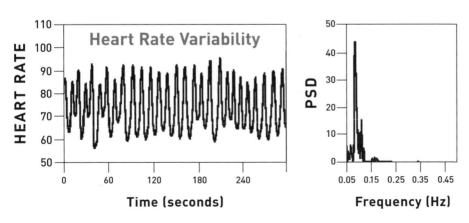

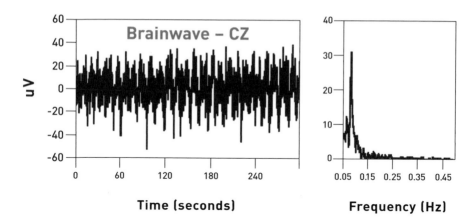

If our children's hearts and emotions are taken care of, their brains will have the chance to develop properly. Healthy *heart rhythms* mean healthy *neurological* development.

I believe that this has profound consequences for *how* we parent and teach our children.

It's not a touchy-feely opinion that the emotional state of a parent has a direct effect on a baby's cognitive function and development. We, as parents, *are* the emotional environment surrounding our babies. If this is true, then it's a terrifying and stressful thought: work stress, arguing-with-your-spouse stress, financial stress, emotional distress, the whole laundry list of stresses, are going to have a *measurable* impact on the neural development of our children. Is there a moment in the day when we aren't being assaulted by some of these?

In light of the following evidence, those old clichés of independence, early literacy, socialisation, etc., which have become the myths we bandy about in parent groups all over the world as essential for young children, dissolve into irrelevance pretty quickly once we realise what's really important.

KEY POINTS

- The right thing at the right time makes all the difference.

- Letting babies cry themselves to sleep raises cortisol levels even when they stop crying.

- Environments continue to have a profound effect on children's heart and brain rhythms after they leave the womb.

- Loving touch is the most important ingredient in healthy emotional, physiological and cognitive development.

- As parents, we *are* the emotional environment surrounding our babies.

STARTING TO EXPLORE: EARLY CHILDHOOD

Hearts have a deep metaphorical significance in all cultures across the world. And it's no wonder. Love is a powerful force. But metaphorically speaking, our collective worldwide hearts in general are not at ease. We're living in a state of global dis-ease. And passing it on to the next generation.

Quite practically, if we allow our hearts to experience enough positive and loving emotions, we have a good chance of extending our lives and the lives of the people we love. The heart has a powerful electrical field that has been measured to extend about 3 square feet (0.3m^2) around each person. The heart's electrical field interacts with the brain and has a synchronising effect. Research shows that when a person is in a state of *heart* rhythm coherence, their *brainwaves* can synchronise to another person's heartbeat.

A mother nursing her baby in a high state of coherence, feeling love and appreciation, entrains her baby's brainwaves to her heart rhythm patterns. A stressed mother entrains a child into a state of stress. So, don't be thinking about that blocked drain or stressing about the high phone bill while you're nursing!

Children, as they grow and are held close to a loving parent or caregiver, become accustomed to the heart rhythm pattern generated by that parent. It's very similar to when they were in the womb. That pattern establishes itself as the norm, the baseline, for them. So, it's essential for healthy brain development that primary caregivers are loving and kind, generating a positive coherent heart rhythm pattern.

If, as we know, the prefrontal cortex is going through a rapid development phase between birth and age three, the consequences of the state of *our* hearts on *their* brains are significant. This finding is discussed in detail in an article entitled 'What New Research on the Heart and Brain Tells Us about Our Youngest Children', by Dr Karl Pribram (MD, PhD) and Deborah Rozman (PhD), which was presented at the White House Conference on Early Childhood Development and Learning. It tells us that brain development, intelligence and emotional skills in young children are inextricably linked to the heart.[8]

The messaging system from the heart to the brain is a complex process. That's why introducing the alphabet to your three-year-old cannot compete with kisses and cuddles in terms of enabling your child to be an emotionally well-balanced, academic genius by the time they turn eighteen. An ounce of emotion, according to the IHM, is worth a pound of repetition.[9]

We know now that there is a physiological state in which all systems are operating at their optimum capacity. In other words, if we can be likened to a violin, we can say there is a point, after some tweaking and tuning, where all four strings are at perfect pitch. Then music can be played and it will all be in tune if the musician knows what to do.

There is a point at which all physiological systems also resonate at their most favourable levels — a point at which blood flow to the brain is optimised, we're not stressed, immune system function is enhanced, we feel happy, and our thoughts are clear as a result. We are generating, from our hearts, an electromagnetic field that is 'coherent' — ordered and harmonious. This is the state of 'high coherence' referred to earlier.

We are the musicians and also the instruments — and we have the capacity to tune our bodies. For the sake of our children, we should aim to be in that tuned state as much as possible.

Experiments at the IHM have shown that a person standing within 4 feet (1.2m) of someone else can affect the brainwaves of the other by generating a highly coherent heart rhythm pattern. And remember, we can't fake it. Our hearts always detect the real signal. In our children's early years, our response is especially crucial. While you can't pretend everything's okay while you freak out that your four-year-old has just run into a birdbath and split the skin open under his eye, you can hold him to you and talk quietly and breathe deeply yourself. It will help him (and you) to calm down.

If, as parents and caregivers, our instruments are out of tune, even if we pretend that all is well, our disharmony cannot be concealed and it will affect our children as their electromagnetic fields decode information generated by ours.

The following diagram shows how our hearts generate a large electromagnetic field that affects and is affected by other electromagnetic fields, especially those generated by other people's hearts.[10]

THE HEART'S ELECTROMAGNETIC FIELD

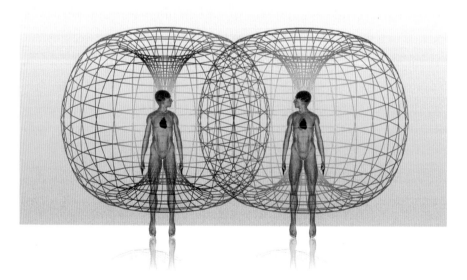

The autonomic nervous system adapts itself to the pattern of either coherence or incoherence when children are young and brains are developing. Is it possible that the rapid rise in ADHD and other behaviour disorders is a result of mothers being stressed while pregnant, and children being put into day care centres early or left at centres where there might be a very efficient, functional but sterile environment, where there is no opportunity to develop high physiological coherence patterns?

Most mothers hold their infants on the left-hand side, which is closest to the heart. When a mother is in a loving state, the baby's heart rhythm patterns entrain to their mother's. It's this relationship and feedback pattern, going from the mother's heart to the baby's heart and then to the baby's brain, that becomes the foundation for a child's later emotional and psychological development.

> [T]hrough the development of the far frontal cortex and its connections to the amygdala and perirhinal cortex, *the 'state of the heart' of the primary caregiver becomes important in a child's brain maturation* [emphasis added].
>
> The beneficial effect(s) of loving contact … can be amplified by the adult consciously adopting a more sincere loving or caring emotional state, thus introducing increased coherence into the cardiac field.[11]

This is a key finding from the IHM. When we're close to someone, especially when we are touching or holding someone, the pattern of one person's electrocardiogram (ECG) can be echoed in the other's electroencephalogram (EEG). The effect is strongest when we touch, but if we are both are in a state of 'high coherence' even just being near each other has a similar effect.

Imagine the implications for how we'd parent our young children if they were hooked up to sensors that displayed their heart rhythms (as they would be if they were premature babies in a neonatal unit). We can't see how their heart rhythms are reacting to their environments and the people in them, but if we could, would we modify our responses? Would we change the physical environment?

If we soften the environments our small children live in, lower our voices, breathe deeply ourselves and try to listen carefully to what their growing bodies are telling us, we might begin to prevent some of the reactive things we do in the heat of our stressful lives and which impact our children for the rest of theirs.

I've been so inspired by the research at the IHM that I've brought it into my home and teaching life as much as possible. Some years ago, when my son was going through a very anxious time at school and had trouble falling asleep, he would say, 'Can you lie next to me and make me relax?' And I would snuggle up to him, breathe slowly and deeply and consciously adopt that sincere, loving state that's not at all difficult to do when it's your child ... and within a few minutes he'd be fast asleep. I did that for several nights in a row and he came through his struggle in one piece.

Our young children can't ask us to do these things. We need to just do them. There probably isn't a single parent who hasn't had their child lose it badly in some public place. A parent is in the middle of the cereal aisle when suddenly their little one, who has been an angelic cherub for two years, turns into a two-foot tyrant with an apparently malicious agenda. The tyrant appears to be demanding one thing after another, and after the parent's numerous refusals, is going for the meltdown. Well, that's how it seems, anyway. Other customers look on in sympathy or annoyance or disdain, and then, in most cases, the parent raises his or her voice above the little tyrant's and yells.

Or worse. I've seen more exasperated slaps than I'd care to count.

So, what's really going on here, and is there any other possible outcome?

First of all, for someone who has only been in the world a few years, a mall or any kind of shopping environment where there are twenty aisles of different things, bright lights, music blaring, and loudspeakers announcing great deals on instant soup, this scenario constitutes sensory overload. A two-year-old might manage this overload for ten or fifteen minutes, but after 45? Forget it. So, what can we do, because we have to get the shopping done?

Contrary to all appearances, our child is not a two-foot tyrant with a malicious agenda; she's an overwhelmed little person, and her nervous system cannot cope with the assault on her senses. Our best bet might be to decide to go shopping after her nap and a snack, when the stores are quieter and we can get through it more quickly. It takes a bit of planning and is not always so convenient, but sometimes it's worth it. And then, as we go, we need to keep watch, take note of the signs of stress: restlessness, tearfulness, demanding things — all these are indicators that her heart rate is increasing, stress hormones are being released, and she doesn't know what to do with it all. The last thing we need, as a parent, is another stressed-out nervous system in her vicinity. Ours. So even as she frets, if we start to breathe deeply, quietly, grasp for those thoughts of gratitude, and lower our voice rather than raise it, she will be helped.

Having her demands for new toys met is not what she's really asking for. She wants to be taken out of the situation that's overwhelming her, emotionally and physically. Her heart rate is likely to be as rapid as a hunted deer's, her face is red and she's sweating and flailing her arms around. A soft hand on her head, a whisper in her ear, will do more for her (and for you) than a swift slap on the leg or the purchase of another toy. She might not be able to calm right down, since overdrive is overdrive, but if we can't avoid getting into the situation, we can always avert a catastrophe.

In my experience, this goes for all temper tantrums and meltdowns. My child, with his hypersensitivity (or sensory integration issues) was my best teacher. He could actually sustain a crying tantrum for two hours. When other children were just getting started at the playground or at someone's house, he was already done and had reached melting point. I was exhausted, but I only descended to his level of hysteria once or twice — and regretted it. Once, when he was three, I suddenly yelled at him to stop screaming. (Great examples we are sometimes.) His whole body jerked as though I'd physically shocked him. He stared at me with wide eyes and said, 'You did the wrong thing.' Tell me about it! Soon after that, it happened again. I couldn't stand another second of his tantrum and made my voice louder than his screams so that he stopped mid-breath. He looked at me with tears still glistening on his eyelashes and said, 'I didn't know it was so hard for you.'

He remembers both those occasions. After that, I got wise. Next tantrum (the cause is always irrelevant; you know that, right?) I put my hand softly on his head and said, 'It's very noisy for me here, so I'm just going into the bathroom for some quiet. I love you and I'll come out when it's not so loud.' I locked myself in the bathroom and he threw himself against the door and was loud for another ten torturous minutes while I breathed deeply and calmly, and continued to love my child. Eventually he stopped. 'It's not loud anymore,' he said. It was as if he observed the whole scenario from the outside. As though he couldn't help what was happening to his body. I came out and gave him a big hug. 'Let's go and read a story,' I said. End of story. End of tantrum. I thought it was the end of me too, I was so exhausted, but it was part of my learning process: if I didn't want to live in a stressed-out house where people yelled and doors slammed, I knew I had to start at the beginning. My son is now a mellow and well-adjusted teen. People often ask us why we didn't have ten kids, and I've stopped explaining that for many years I felt like I *did* have ten. A lot of struggle and inner searching and experimenting went on in those years.

When children lose their bearings in the world, it's of utmost importance that we, firstly, don't give in to permissive parenting, which is the equivalent of zero support for someone who is about to collapse, and that we, secondly, don't revert to autocracy. There is a firm and kind road across even territory that makes our children feel loved and secure, while showing them exactly where the boundaries are.

Let's imagine then that early childhood (before children start school) is a slow moving out into the world for our children. The more gradual the process away from the womb, the greater the chance the nervous system will develop in a healthy way.

At this stage children love to explore and see what happens when their bodies interact with their environment. They need to be able to open cupboards and climb things and feel textures. If we watch them and support them, not letting them get into danger but not shouting 'no' to their desire to know their world, we're helping brains and bodies develop. Watch what a small child naturally loves to do and it's not hard to see what part of their physiology is involved.

Imagine our five-year-old keeps turning on the garden hose to see it rear up like a live snake as water powerfully rushes through. We've already said no, and so his continuation (despite our cross face) looks a lot like civil disobedience. Either he is naughty, rebellious and wasteful or this is a moment of such intense delight and discovery for him that he cannot tear himself away. It's the physics he's after: look at what water can do when the force is channelled into a narrow place! So, before our frowns deepen, we might stay for a moment. Check it out. See it for the first time. Maybe do it ourselves. Admire the force of water. Then we might suggest filling a watering can and bringing some of that to the flowers at the back of the house. We've just taken a 'no!' moment, a potential stressor, and transformed it.

When I'm around groups of parents in parks or shopping centres, I'm always stunned at the amount of 'Stop that!' and 'Get over here!' and 'No!' and 'I told you not to!' I hear. No wonder our children grow up feeling misunderstood. We have to begin by understanding that a pre-schooler climbing on the furniture *needs* to climb. It's his physiological development at stake. If we don't want him ruining the best couch, we should get some climbing equipment. He'll be smarter and more emotionally well adjusted if we do.

This is not the equivalent of permissive parenting; we have to be wide awake so that when something important is happening, we don't impose our adult values and expect that our young children have the same intellectual and emotional capacity as we have. They don't. They're not small versions of adults. They're completely different to adults in profound and essential ways. Everything about them is still a magnificent work in progress — bodies, feelings and, most critically, brains are all under construction.

Margie was sick and tired of telling her five-year-old, Jethro, to stop throwing stones and small rocks. He'd hit his brother already on the back by accident and she'd punished him. He still didn't get it and now she was sure he just wanted to annoy her and get her attention. What, after all, is so hard to understand about 'Don't throw stones!'? As adults, we might wonder. But for Jethro, the experiment, the excitement of throwing something and watching the energy from his arm make that stone go way up into the sky, was more compelling than the command to 'Stop that!' He needed to learn that about his environment.

So, what do we do when our child is being dangerous with small rocks and other potential life-enders? It's a question worth asking, because if we wear out that hysterical, high stress 'NO!' (which is necessary for those very rare occasions when, without it, a true disaster or life-ender might ensue) our child becomes immune to it and we have nowhere to go from there. One possibility is to set up a target (quickly). A simple tower of three small rocks will do. Then, we can easily explain how the target is far away from people so they don't get hurt. We can make a show of checking that no one is in harm's way. We can't just *tell* him to look around. We have to *do* it too. Then we could be the first to throw our rock at the target. This is the trick of Harnessing and Directing Energy, as opposed to always having to stop it. Before the age of seven our children are great imitators, so this kind of thing can really work (as opposed to when they're fourteen … when it won't). This is the best time to set a good example. It creates harmony in our relationship with our child, and forms the basis for a loving and stress-less relationship that we will have as a stable island when the high tides of adolescence arrive and threaten to suck everyone out to sea.

In the first few years of our children's lives, while they are still busy building their bodies and learning how to use them, we've got a whole wave of popular culture that tells us to ignore the fundamental emotional and physiological needs of our growing children. We give in to pressures and expose our children to so much that causes them unnecessary stress.

Our impulse to protect our children, to give them the best possible chance in life, has been hijacked. Somehow, 'success' has become synonymous with being academically bright and earning lots of money. We all know, firstly, that money, while it can make things easier, is not a prerequisite for happiness. In the happiness index, developed countries don't come very high on the list.

What about our children's overall health? I'm not talking coughs and colds and stomach bugs. As we push our children to 'succeed' we truly forget about their health, and how pushing them to 'succeed' can affect their health. Is it more important to be successful and rich at 40 and die of a heart attack or to be relaxed, healthy and happy? Do the details (successful, owns own company, respected by many, etc.) really matter in the end? The way we act, it seems we do think it matters. But does it? And do high scores and good grades guarantee financial success?

I ask these rhetorical questions because the way we behave in today's society makes me think we've mostly lost the plot. We assume that a) children must learn to read as early as possible because b) they will be ahead of the academic game in preschool and then c) they will get into a gifted program at elementary and high school and then d) they will graduate with top marks so that they can e) get into a top tier university/competitive business school/etc. which will hopefully guarantee that f) they will be financially successful which will mean g) they will be ultimately happy.

Really?

I recently asked the Year 9s I teach in Australia what they thought their parents wanted for them. Here are some of their answers.

- I think my parents want me to be happy. But not just stupidly happy. They want me to be doing something that makes me happy. Something meaningful for me.

- I think my parents want me to be miserable. They don't care what I do. They want me to have a horrible life and suffer.

- My parents don't mind what I do. They want me to be fulfilled.

- My parents want me to go into business so that I can be financially stable and take care of myself.

Happiness, fulfilment and health are not a guaranteed outcome if we follow the trajectory of early academic testing and buy the stressful myth that being 'smart' and getting good grades will ultimately lead to those outcomes.

We are in danger of destroying childhood with adult stresses and expectations. The magic of childhood, of everything being new and discoverable, of being open and full of wonder, is a small window that closes all too soon and that we cannot go back to for the rest of our lives.

Sometimes our most treasured memories are from childhood, but our deepest traumas reside there too. It's our job as parents and teachers to stop the 'crimes' that we keep committing against our children, robbing them of a precious few years by saturating their world with the grim pressures and stresses of adult life. The truth is, we might not be able to ensure that our children develop into healthy, fulfilled and happy adults, but we can always work on being more conscious and proactive, rather than reactive, when we parent.

Po Bronson and Ashley Merryman's book *NurtureShock*, which explores some of our parenting assumptions that are sometimes really off the mark, provides information on schools in the US where children are being tested for their IQ and academic abilities as young as twenty months. Even at four, the children who score highly on these tests are put into gifted programs, when the proof shows that there is no continuity at all between the supposedly gifted four-year-old and a super-smart eighth-grader. Imagine you've only been out of your mother's womb for twenty months in what will probably be a 90-year life and someone is testing you to decide whether you can go into the smart-box! And to what end? Do these parents ever ask that question? And even if you do seriously need to have a smart child for your own vicarious satisfaction, the great irony is that a loving, low-stress environment with a loving carer is going to be more conducive to emotional and academic success than all the gifted programs put together.

We've become so obsessed with an illusory idea of what 'success' means that we've lost sight of the journey of childhood. This journey will indeed influence the adults our children will become. But the more we impose adult expectations on our children, the more damage we cause — because our children are still works-in-progress. Everything is still forming — bodies, feelings, thoughts. Nothing is complete.

So, we get that we can't stand a three- or four-month-old on his feet and expect him to hold himself up. It's going to take time before his muscles are sufficiently developed, before he has any kind of co-ordination. So, why do we expect our two-year-olds to understand cause and effect? (*No, you can't come with me to the supermarket, because last time you didn't behave and I told you what would happen if you threw another tantrum.*)

The purpose of childhood is *not to arrive at adulthood prematurely*. It is a process of growth that we need to learn to support so that it happens in the most beneficial way to that individual. Then we will have adults emerging who have the *capacity* to create the lives that they want to live, out of their own sense of joy and purpose.

In the first few years of life, parents and the home environment play a large part in our children's development. The scary but inspiring reality is that our emotional state as parents has a measurable impact on our children's development.

KEY POINTS

- The pathway of early learning goes from the parent/caregiver's heart to the baby's heart to the brain.

- Minimise overall stress by staying calm when children are stressed.

- Achieving high coherence can result in ordered, harmonious brainwave patterns in ourselves but also, most importantly, in our children.

- Loving touch is the most important ingredient in healthy emotional, physiological and cognitive development.

- We should parent as though we were watching our children's ECG patterns on a heart monitor.

OFF TO SCHOOL:
AGES SIX AND UP

In light of the fact that from about age six onwards many children spend most of their waking hours at school, the educational setting is bound to impact our children's bodies. The very same elements that were true concerning the effect of the home environment and the emotional state of the parent/caregiver on small children apply when those children go to school.

Their heart rhythms are still changing throughout the day in response to the environment that surrounds them — only we parents don't see it. We only experience the 'before' and 'after', and we make our judgement on whether our children are thriving at school based on either groans or excitement in the morning, and the same behaviour at the end of the day.

If one person's coherent heart rhythms can impact another's brainwave patterns, and if a loving parent at home can support a child's developing physiological, emotional and cognitive patterns, it follows that when our children go to school, they are going to be affected by the teachers in the room and the physical environment of the school. I'd suggest that it's a really important factor whether teachers are harmoniously, appreciatively involved in their student's development or whether they merely *act* as if they are. If children spend the day with angry or stressed teachers, even if these teachers don't show it, this has an effect.

The emotional state of the adult in any educational environment is still potentially 'contagious' to the children in that environment.

The brain has not stopped developing. Children are involved, especially in the primary school years, with the busy work of building their bodies, producing new teeth, new neural networks and reaching other important physiological milestones. We need to understand that by observing what children do and what's happening to their bodies we can get an indication of what they're ready for. If children can play sequential games, use scissors, balance on a low wall or a tree log and hop on one leg, there's a good chance that neural networks are now sheathed with myelin, and conductivity is increased, so that learning to read and write will be a natural step in their development. Stress emerges when we insist that all children should be at the same developmental phase at exactly the same age, and we don't take into account that when a child indicates that learning to read is painful and near impossible, there may be a very real, physiological reason. Schools that understand the importance of meeting children *where they are at* — and teachers who do not threaten their students with failure if they don't meet certain standards — create a foundation for optimum learning. The teacher's state of heart is as important as any curriculum.

And then there's touch. In the US, the issue of touch is often taboo. At schools we learn not to touch each other, and certainly teachers do not touch children. 'Keep your hands to yourself!' echoes across the nation's schoolyards. In an effort to be vigilant about abuse and help children to protect themselves, touch has become a definite no-no. It's easy to see how in some societies, for example in the US, we do wonders to both criminalise and sexualise the idea of touch, even though decades of research shows that when the need for touch is not met, abnormal behaviour ensues. It is deeply entrenched in the culture and absorbed by parents and children alike: *don't touch yourself, don't touch others, don't let others touch you.* The idea of course, is protective, but the result is that when super-vigilance leads to touch being perceived as inherently dangerous, there are very real and negative consequences. In the UK and Australia, it hasn't permeated general society to such a degree, but we are inheriting aspects of the perception of touch as negative and we would do well to guard against it making further inroads. Harlow's cruel monkey experiments resulted in the confirmation that monkeys deprived of touch developed sociopathic and other aberrant behaviours, showing a long time ago that touch was essential for healthy development.

When we look at educational and care-giving environments, in addition to looking at the facility, the mission statement and the academic achievement scores, we should meet the people who will be spending the best part of the day with our child. The teacher's state of heart may well be an important influence on how well and how happily our children learn.

Before birth, and just after, high heart rate variability (HRV) in babies is associated with a thriving individual, while low variability signals distress. Extensive HRV research concludes that, in children and adults, high HRV is a sign of thriving individuals. Low HRV, especially in children, is often predictive of ADHD and other behaviour disorders. In addition, we saw earlier that not only are we able to change our brainwaves by how *we* feel, but we can have a measurable effect on the brainwaves of those around us. The implications for this in our educational environments are enormous.

For example, are there educational environments that, because of how they are set up, might introduce increased coherence into a child's cardiac field, and consequently, into the brain's electrical field? Would children learn better, and perform better academically, if they were given the opportunity to generate coherent heart rhythm patterns during the day? And when we're looking at schools for our children, should we consider whether a school will generate a positive emotional state, and thus support our children's nervous, immune and hormonal systems?

I'm convinced that children are being profoundly affected by their classroom environments and the teachers who teach there, and that these effects are measurable. I'm also convinced that certain environments are more beneficial than others to a child's cognitive, emotional and physiological development, and that, as parents, we should be able to walk into a school and ask a few fundamental questions to determine whether we feel the school and teachers will support our child's physical, emotional and academic development.

I recently visited some public schools in the US state of Florida to observe what atmosphere pervades the mainstream school environment in America, where millions of children spend an average of seven hours per day.

The first school was an elementary school in Sarasota. In the Kindergarten room, the ceiling buzzed with fluorescent lights. A TV was loudly broadcasting an onsite educational program, simultaneously showing in all the Kindergarten rooms down the hall, so that the voice on the screen echoed through the corridor like an image in a never-ending hall of mirrors. The teacher was trying to talk to the students over this. The walls were covered in words and shapes and information. After ten minutes, I had to wonder whether this environment was trying to meet the short attention spans of ADHD children or whether it could be blamed for helping to create ADHD patterns in children. Certainly I could not find where to place my focus and was grateful that I wasn't spending the day in that room.

I observed how the teacher was struggling to make her voice heard above the other noise, how scattered and noisy and adversarial the children were, and how the teacher did not seem particularly happy to be at work that day. I couldn't blame her one bit.

In the next Kindergarten, the teacher had the TV off. She was reading her group a story and it was evident that she was happy to be at work that day, that her children were excited to see her. She had a fish tank in the room and the children took turns feeding the fish. She told me that her class was the odd one out in the school. They were the happy, 'naughty' ones who were determined to have fun despite what she called the damaging and upsetting institutionalisation of a punishment-and-reward system. She said that when her children came in from other classes she had to have discussions with them when they were upset about the rewards system. She would have to comfort them and help them feel that they had support, so that even if the science teacher only gave one award to one student, she, the main teacher, would tell them that they all deserved awards. Same fluorescent lights, same walls of information, but an altogether different 'vibe' existed in her room.

I then visited a 'gifted' second grade. The fluorescent lights attracted more than their fair share of my attention, since I personally find it distracting to work in neon-lit areas. Several computer screens were emitting different noises, but the atmosphere was pleasant. The teacher seemed relaxed. She shared with me that teaching the gifted second graders was her favourite job. They didn't have to worry about upcoming FCATs (Florida's Comprehensive Assessment Tests). That fear belonged to the fourth-grade teachers, two of whom I would meet later that day. This class was extremely capable and they all went to different 'work stations' to do what was required of them. The children seemed mostly content and got along well with one another.

My next visit was to a school on Anna Maria Island in Florida, where the fourth-grade was getting ready for the FCATs. Under the legislation in place, every school gets a grade. If your school fails, everything is affected, from programs to funding to a teacher's contract. Your job as a teacher is to make sure that your children pass. If your class gets a 'bad' grade, the school's grade is affected and your job as a teacher may well be on the line. So, you are depending on your children to 'make it' for their sake, the school's sake, and your sake. No pressure here. (Although the FCATs are soon to be phased out, they will simply be replaced by a more rigorous nationally standardised test, which will do nothing to alleviate stress or stop teachers 'teaching to the test'.)

The teachers were kind and intelligent. 'Look at these children,' one said. 'They are all going to be burned out. They come into fourth grade barely able to do long division and I have to get them to where they can calculate all this.' She showed me a page from a mock test that would have to be successfully managed by the class. 'We don't even have time for recess in the day because we just have to get them through these tests. They're lucky if they get fifteen minutes outside between 8 a.m. and 3 p.m.'

The teacher was stressed. The class was stressed. If we were really concerned with our children's true and healthy cognitive development and academic achievement, and not with meeting the requirements of current legislation, it might be prudent to just open the doors and let the children out into the sunshine.

In the hills outside a small town called Mullumbimby in New South Wales, Australia, a small primary school seems to have taken some significant steps to support the well-rounded and healthy development of its children, aged five to twelve, or to support, as I would say, the slow maturation of the children's nervous systems. Every Friday, the entire day is dedicated to a non-academic or 'enrichment' program. Children participate in music, sport, art and drama. In addition to this, there are significant breaks during the day throughout the week. Children are outside for half an hour during 'morning tea' time at about 11 a.m., and for 45 minutes during lunch, at about 1 p.m. The principal of the school at the time I visited said she had zero tolerance for bullying and behaviour

issues, and while one of the ways of dealing with that was to not let anyone get away with transgressions, the other was to introduce programs
that actively supported healthy, balanced development. The different
year levels were mixed on a Friday, facilitating healthy social interactions between the older and younger classes as they engaged in music,
drama, art or sport together. The children I met there were exceptionally
polite and well behaved, and the playground at lunchtime resembled a
hive of busy bees. This school, too, had to cope with standardised tests in
years 3 and 5, but unlike the situation in Florida, the focus had not (yet)
shifted from *teaching* children to *testing* them.

Across the world, there are millions of stressed children and teachers. Unfortunately, our ten-year-olds are not hooked up to heart sensors
like they would be if they were premature babies in the neonatal ward.
There is no way of definitively saying that an environment is decidedly
unhealthy and that if the children continue to be impacted like this for
the next eight years there will be negative and even distressing results in
terms of physiological, mental and emotional health.

In our pursuit of so-called academic excellence, everything else has
fallen by the wayside, and a child's health is compromised while we blun-
der on with stone-age tools of earlier and earlier academic assessments,
behaviour evaluations and IQ scores, without understanding that our
children are still developing and the milestones we set are not based on a
sound physiological understanding of that development. The great irony
is that there's a direct correlation between a child's intellectual development and the environment. Either that environment is loving, coherent and supportive of the child's physiological, emotional and cognitive
stage of development, or it isn't. When it isn't, stress is the result.

At the University of London, Dr Hans Eysenck and colleagues have
conducted long-term studies that have shown that 'chronic unmanaged emotional stress is as much as six times more predictive of cancer

and heart disease than cigarette smoking, cholesterol level or blood pressure'.[12]

That's a staggering thought. We try to give our children nutritious food, protect them against sunburn and ensure they don't get too cold or hot. And yet, if we want to protect them against cancer and heart disease, we have to seriously consider the stress we place them under in their home and school environments, and how we mitigate that, or whether we even do. We have to be prepared to ask whether our educational environments are compromising our children's overall health or whether they're actively supporting the development of intelligent, well-adjusted individuals.

If we forget about all our educational and child-rearing theories for a moment and look empirically at children who are just starting school, we can tell a few things: six-year-olds have not yet finished growing; their hands are chubby and their bones are rapidly growing; they have gaps in their mouths where teeth used to be; they have trouble articulating things; they want to move all the time; they get tired and cranky and sometimes they still need to nap; they believe in magic; the world is still a wonderful, mysterious place.

Then we put them in a room with flickering lights, make them sit still in small wooden or plastic chairs from 9 a.m. to 3 p.m., give them worksheets to fill in, teach them their ABCs and give them spelling tests every week to make sure they're learning what we're teaching them. When they don't conform to this new regime all at the same time, we punish and reward them, cajoling them into acquiescence, and if that fails to work, we have them diagnosed with ADHD or learning disabilities and sometimes we medicate them so that they can sit still, 'absorb' information and be 'educated'.

My fear is that too many people in charge of education and curriculum design, parents and teachers, are deeply uneducated about children's physiological, emotional and therefore academic developmental stages. We can't all have degrees in neuroscience before we become teachers or parents, but a few critical bits of information are essential before we subject our children to the rigours of growing up and being educated.

When we look at school-age children, we have to remember that the brain is not a completed organ at birth. In fact, it takes ten to twelve years before we can say that a basic, general stage of brain development has been reached. The different brain regions and connecting neural pathways have to have matured to a certain extent before we can say that cognitive, sensory and motor functions are successfully developed.

Myelin is a fatty insulator that surrounds nerve fibres and allows for smooth transmission of messages between neural networks. Young children's brains are still in the process of being myelinated, and that's why we can't present the criteria for a persuasive argument to a seven-year-old and expect comprehension and why we can easily do that with most sixteen-year-olds. The speed at which the neural networks transport information depends to a large extent on the thickness of the myelin sheath around connecting nerve fibres. There's no hard and fast rule, no timetable for the myelination process through childhood and young adulthood, but what we need to know as parents (and teachers) is that it happens *slowly*.

If we're presenting a seven-year-old with a concept, a problem or even a spelling test which he is not *physiologically* capable of managing, because his particular brain has not matured yet to that extent, we're firmly in the business of causing undue stress (both emotional and physical), which could then easily continue unabated for years to come as that child develops a stress response to spelling or mathematics or academic work in general. If we're trying to reason with our seven-year olds or explain something to them, we have to remember that their brains are not like adult brains at all and that highly intellectual responses to their questions or behaviour are more stressful than helpful.

In Australia, five out of every 100 children apparently have attention deficit disorder. I say 'apparently' because I've had many experiences with ADHD children and my sense is that the problem lies not simply in the child but in the interaction *between* the child and a particular environment. ADHD affects more boys than girls. Boys are often more physically active than girls, which means that they innately require more movement and activity — and which is why they're often more difficult to squash into seats than girls are.

I've been teaching for eighteen years in the US and Australia, and during that time, hundreds of children have passed through my rooms, ranging in age from six to eighteen. I can say without question that at the best of times our youngest school-goers don't easily thrive in closed rooms with small desks, bright lights and lots of 'headwork'.

Consider these signs and symptoms of ADD/ADHD on the website of the Royal Children's Hospital in Melbourne:

- **Inattention:** Difficulty concentrating, forgetting instructions, moving from one task to another without completing anything.

- **Impulsivity:** Talking over the top of others, losing control of emotions easily, being accident prone.

- **Overactivity:** Constant fidgeting and restlessness.

Here's a note from another 'helpful' website about ADHD:

> **'Children with ADD/ADHD can pay attention when they're doing things they enjoy or hearing about topics they enjoy. But when the task is repetitive or boring, they quickly tune out.'**[13]

We're talking *young* children here. Could it be that these children, whose innate development requires them to move and to evolve both gross and fine motor skills, are actually in an environment that by its very nature doesn't properly support them?

Let me share my observation of some of these attention deficit disorder children whom I've had the privilege of teaching: those *specific* problems referred to on the Melbourne children's hospital website dissolve into almost nothing outdoors. I've taken these six- and seven-year-olds who are little menaces in the classroom out into the wild. I've watched them observe a snake eating a frog. I've seen them negotiate their safe passage across a river by stepping on slippery rocks. They had no difficulty concentrating. They didn't stray from their task. They were not restless and fidgety and they didn't lose control of their emotions. So, maybe it's the way our primary-school environment is designed that is simply the wrong fit for a body that needs to engage very actively with the world in a different way, while the brain slowly gains maturity.

Jakob was my student in Sarasota, Florida, when he was seven. He was a ball of energy, unable to sit still; he was bright, chaotic, mischievous and quite a handful. It was a hard thing for him to 'stay on task' in first grade. He was always exploding out of his seat or talking to a friend excitedly about something. But I had to teach him, and for that to happen, he had to be at his desk like everyone else. It was an activity not unlike trying to squash an expansive impulsive genie back into a thin-necked bottle.

But then we went on a beach walk, all the way to the rocks at the end and across them, into tidal pools and onto the slippery areas where the waves were crashing. Jakob was in his element. His clothes got wet faster than anyone else's, but he was completely engaged in his environment. He found live fish, dead fish, starfish. He knew the names of all the fish we saw in the tidal pools. He knew everything about the different anemones and showed his friends how to handle them. In the classroom, I would have checked all the ADHD boxes regarding Jakob. Outside on the beach, I would have checked none of them: he was trustworthy, reliable, knowledgeable, focused and, okay, very muddy.

He was the perfect example of a child telling a teacher in the most basic way possible that he wasn't ready to learn 'sitting still at a desk' for hours a day. He was ready to dive into the world with both hands and learn about his environment. If children 'tune out' when a task is repetitive or boring or not engaging their brains in a developmentally appropriate way, then maybe that 'tuning out' is simply protection. Primary school children *need* to be enjoying everything they do. If they don't feel love for what they're doing or learning, if it isn't an activity that they are physiologically ripe to undertake, they simply won't, or *can't*, learn it. And it will be a stressor on their growing brains and bodies.

Certainly, ADHD is a real issue, but my point is that we often create environments that truly exacerbate the problem. In Australia, a typical day in a public primary school in New South Wales looks somewhat like this:

- 8.45–11 a.m.: Literacy. In this class, everything from spelling to grammar to writing and reading takes place.

- 11–11.30 a.m.: Break

- 11.30 a.m.–12.30 p.m.: Numeracy

- 12.30–1 p.m.: Sport

- 1–1.45 p.m.: Lunch

- 1.45–2.45 p.m.: Literature or Science or Study of Human Society and Environment.

This scenario looks a bit less intensive than the school days in Florida where the children got fifteen minutes outside *if they were lucky*, but the focus is still almost exclusively academic — which, we might think, is what school is all about. However, obviously in order for the best academic results to be gained, the students have to be able to benefit from their learning. Half an hour of sport is a great release, but there's something missing in this picture. The children's academic needs are being met; their physical needs are too, to a degree. But there's an entire spectrum that is left out of the curriculum, one that researchers in Australia at least are finally identifying and trying to integrate back into the curriculum. When the arts are part of the curriculum, researchers have found that academic success ensues, as does emotional balance.

Most schools focus on addressing academics as a priority, and perhaps, if it's a good school, even ensuring students get enough physical exercise. That certainly addresses the head and the limbs, but the 'heart' is not being fed. If we neglect their metaphorical and physical hearts throughout children's school years, they are potentially at risk of becoming diseased. There has to be cognitive, emotional and physical balance in the way children are educated in order for them to thrive later in these areas. If cognition engages the head, and physical activity, the limbs, then emotion engages the heart. We can't ignore the significance of the arts in any curriculum.

If our children are relentlessly under pressure to perform academically, their brains are often not in an optimum state to process whatever learning is supposed to be happening. It's exhausting both physically and mentally to go from one academic hour to another throughout the day without a complete change in rhythm.

Of course, we do all have to master the skills that will eventually enable us to navigate the modern world, so what can possibly be done differently to make a learning environment more conducive to, well, learning? The truth is that it's *how* and *when* we do something that can make the critical difference between being stressed to death or arriving at the brink of adulthood with the necessary tools to take on the challenges life throws our way.

KEY POINTS

- The teacher's state of heart affects the students.

- Children who exhibit behaviour issues often have low heart rate variability and struggle to adapt to the small changes that occur throughout the day.

- A stressful classroom environment affects children's hearts and nervous systems.

- Sustaining positive feeling states can counter and change the effects of stress.

- A good curriculum supports physical, emotional and cognitive development in equal measure.

- Stress arises when a child is not physiologically developed enough to meet the requirements of the task.

EMERGING ADULTS:
THE TEENAGE YEARS

Just as little children are not miniature adults, so teens are not merely adults with faulty risk-assessment hardware. They are a delicate and unique species, and the world they have to negotiate is unbelievably complex and fast moving.

A 2007 article by Carol Midgley, called 'Young and Desperate', which was published in *The Times,* in London, focused on the current plight of teens in the UK, where the overriding theme seems to be that youngsters are experiencing an overwhelming disconnect. British studies, Midgley says, indicate that about 10 per cent of five- to sixteen-year-olds suffer from behaviour issues, and that the number of children on anti-depressants has risen by 70 per cent over the past two decades. This doesn't mean that *depression* is on the rise necessarily, only that the use of anti-depressants is. This is disturbing, given that teen brains are going through a fairly rapid pruning phase and that neurological development is not at all complete.

The Times asked depressed teens to write in and tell their stories. Many teens wrote in to say that the most depressing aspect of their lives was the message they received from parents, teachers and peers that they were not okay as they were. Parents, the article revealed, were pushy and often wanted to fulfil themselves through their children's achievements.

The fact that many teens are on anti-depressants unsettles Professor David Healy, a consultant psychiatrist at Cardiff University College of Medicine, quoted in the article. He doesn't believe there's an increase in depression. And he is reticent about dishing out pills so readily to youngsters whose 'brains are still taking shape'.

Depression results from unreasonable expectations combined with unmanageable amounts of stress. During the teen years, the prefrontal cortex goes through another rapid development phase, equalled only by the one experienced in early childhood. If teens are severely depressed, we might ask why. What's missing in the cyber-world of virtual relationships, online chat, Skype, iPads, text messaging and school stress?

Michael Conner, an American clinical psychologist, author and expert in crisis intervention, states that while some youngsters have more of a vulnerability to it, 'depression is almost always caused by society, not the brain'.[14] Who makes up the society that surrounds these teens? At home it's family. At school, teachers and friends. And media is definitely causing a disconnect:

> **The texting and virtual friendships that happen**
> **on Facebook and in chat rooms add to stress and**
> **afflict young people. Teens complain of a massive**
> **disconnect, a feeling of worthlessness and**
> **pointlessness ... they are getting twenty messages**
> **a day and spending hours in front of a screen.**
> **Teenagers seem to be very aware of the wider world**
> **these days, but not very self-aware.[15]**

That's cause for concern. If we look at all the potential stressors in a young person's life, the negative aspects of society, which may include parental and peer pressure, rejection, abuse, neglect and not feeling 'good enough' for the adults in their environments — this can all lead to depression. It seems, though, that school stress and parental stress regarding school performance has a significant impact on how young adults respond to their world.

The reason some teens are more susceptible than others to depression has a lot to do with earlier environments. Background and the stress response are important. If a child has grown up with loving, open, supportive parents or caregivers who have either consciously or unconsciously created a relaxed and accepting environment, the physiology and brain structure of that teen will be in better shape than the teen who has grown up with stress, misunderstanding, fear of punishment and pressure to be something other than what they are.

The stresses that we experience, says Michael Conner, 'change our physiology, which causes our genes to produce proteins that actually change the function and structure of our brain. This creates physical and psychological symptoms that can last a lifetime.'[16] We already know this about the development of a child's brain and how stress can create patterns of response in us even before we're born.

It's a fact. The longer we're exposed to stress from the beginning of our lives, the more our physiology, in particular our brain, is changed.

So, what protection is there when the world seems to be such a stressful place? After all, stress is apparently an unavoidable part of being human. The good news is that at every step along the way, as our children grow, there are ways of mitigating that stress, of giving our children a 'safe verandah' so that the nervous system is not in a constant state of fight-or-flight. The first clue as to how teen stress and depression can be minimised lies in early childhood.

When I was teaching the early grades in the US, I often heard parents saying that it's not worth overprotecting children because 'it's a tough world out there'. As I've said before, the surprising reality — which is hopefully becoming obvious in this book — is that if the tough world is causing stress, the *earlier* our children are exposed to it, the *worse* it is for them, for their brains and their health.

In fact, the longer we protect our young children from stress and anxiety, the healthier their stress responses will be, and the more resilient they will be when they do encounter stress. Then, when these children arrive in high school and have to deal with all kinds of new and sometimes disturbing realities, their own responses to everything from exam stress to offers of illicit drugs will be infused with a degree of equilibrium.

Extensive work by brain researcher and neurosurgeon Dr Karl Pribram has helped to advance the understanding of the emotional system. It seems familiar patterns from the external environment and from within the body are ultimately written into neural circuitry.[17] If a child is exposed early to stressful situations he is emotionally or physically not equipped to handle, the responses that he develops become a blueprint for responses later on. Your teenager is a result of the child he was ten years previously.

Trying to 'unwrite' stress responses set up in early years is a very difficult task. It's so much easier to not set up an over-active stress response in our children to begin with, but even with teens who are already stressed, there is a lot we can do to minimise the effects of that stress so that it does not become an overwhelming factor in their lives. Once we understand how a child's response to the immediate familiar environment becomes a pattern in that child's neural circuitry, we can be protective and pro-active parents. 'Children can be protected from potential stressors by certain "buffers" such as a functional family, friends, recreation, adventure, creativity, and sleep.'[18]

And touch. We know how touching someone when both people are in a state of 'high coherence' can lead to the onset of alpha rhythms in one person's brainwave patterns as a response to another's 'coherent' heart rhythms. Touch is critical to emotional health. Most little children love being cuddled by their parents. Most teens don't! If you get your hugs and kisses while they are still being given freely, it will be a lot easier to steal one now and again from your gangly fourteen-year-old.

Could it be possible that premature sexual relationships are the result of a desperate craving for touch, as teens make their way in a world that increasingly isolates them physically from one another, their families and themselves?

Behavioural problems correlate directly with intense sympathetic nervous system activity, and a pattern of 'incoherence' is often established in the early years, between birth and three, when the prefrontal cortex is experiencing its first most rapid development period. So the environment surrounding the three-year-old is going to create the patterns that may determine how the same child as a seventeen-year-old will respond to the many stressors in their environment, and whether that teen becomes depressed or exhibits other behaviour issues.

At this time, when the prefrontal cortex is going through its next rapid growth period, the preceding information makes me think that it's of prime importance whether these teens are in a loving, caring and intelligent environment with people who themselves are full of genuine compassion and interest, or not.

In a study of 138 children in the US, researchers found that it wasn't only the children's *exposure* to stress but also their bodies' *reactions* to the stress that affected their future behaviour. Young children who had both a stressful home life and an exaggerated nervous system response to stress were more likely than their peers to develop behavioural problems over the next six years.

The findings suggest that children with greater nervous system reactivity have a particular need to be shielded from chronic stress, lead study author Daniel Hart told *Reuters Health*. 'What some kids can shrug off [may] be harmful to others,' explained Hart, a psychologist at the Center for Children and Childhood Studies at Rutgers University in Camden, New Jersey.

In their ongoing research, Hart said, he and his colleagues have found that when children who are prone to greater stress reactions do not have chronic stress in their lives, they 'may really flourish'.[19]

Indeed.

In a recent conversation with a couple of Australian thirteen-year-olds, I asked them what the most stressful part of their lives was at the moment.

'Homework and assignments,' said one. 'I get so stressed having all these deadlines and mountains of work that I have to finish. And I have to do it all, because I want to get good grades. There's no time to go outside or relax or go to the beach.'

'Yeah, it's pretty stressful,' said the other. 'Teachers have no idea how much work the other teachers give us. They just each pile on the work.'

'And it's, like, you only get one chance. You have to get a good OP score if you want to get into a good university. I don't know what I want to study, so I need to do well at everything so that I can have a choice. You only get this one chance and then that's it. You're set for life.'

I'm pretty sure that they're speaking for what the majority of students, teachers and parents believe. You've got this one chance: somewhere in the future is a date with your name on it. When you reach that date and take your final exam, in whichever country, your results will determine whether you will be a success or a failure in the world. This is it. The make-or-break moment you've been trained for since you were twenty months old. One of my Year 11 students, who is sixteen, recently said to me, 'I'm so scared of next year. I have no idea what I want to do or be and everyone keeps asking me what my plans are.'

We've created an entire culture that believes in this premise: you have *one* shot at it. And it's my belief that this fallacy is the cause of most of the stress we as parents and educators impose on children throughout their school years.

In reality, in Australia, there are at least 43 different pathways to university, if that's what you want. And of course, the world is full of self-made millionaires and businesspeople and stars and successful and creative and happy people of all kinds who never made it through high school. Not that I'm advocating not making it through high school. I'm just unpacking this strange myth that school-leaving exams define a person for life and predict the success or failure of the next 70 years of existence. It is this assumption that causes parents and teachers so much stress and which we filter down to the students and very young children in our care.

We set up a life-or-death scenario, a fight-or-flight trajectory into which they are locked until they make it (or don't) across the imaginary finish line.

A teenager who commits suicide rather than fail an exam sees a life ahead in which a poor exam result will condemn him to some kind of eternal failure. It's a tough choice: life as a total failure … or death. And the ironic thing is that most of us who are in our thirties and forties have moved so many light years away from who we were at seventeen. We may have lost any school-leaving exam results or not even remember them. We may even have had three or four careers. I have no idea where my South African Matric exam results are. I can't even remember what I got for Geography or for Art, but I do remember how I almost failed Maths, and I do remember the terrible skin outbreaks, the hypoglycaemia, the exhaustion and the late nights that preceded the exam-infested month of November. Never during my initial degree, or during my Masters or Doctorate, did I ever feel so depressed or stressed as I did in that last year of school. I might have lost my Matric certificate but the memory of the stress is written into my physiology.

As parents, we naturally want our children to 'make it'. To be successful at school means our teens need to be academically proficient and meet the expected standards. And there really doesn't seem to be any way around it: to find out how our teens are doing intellectually and academically, we have to test and evaluate them. But we do this mostly out of fear. We're afraid for their future, for our future.

So, instead of looking at the role stress plays in the learning process, we evolve more and more complex systems of measuring everything. And as we uncover problems, we conveniently label children, get more adept and proficient at evaluating, and then we provide special and extensive services to help our children perform better academically. Stress becomes an acceptable, even necessary, reality of life as we push our children towards success. No pain, no gain — we think.

And yet it's no secret that in mainstream education in many developed countries, problems are increasing, standards are falling and tests are getting more profuse in an attempt to 'leave no child behind'. Academics are introduced earlier and earlier, in the hope that this might go some way towards addressing the current crisis in education.

It's my assertion that not only different forms of education but the whole educational environment can have a profound, *measurable* effect on the intellectual, emotional and physiological development of children. And we often aren't taking that into account. But somewhere in the world, thankfully, they are: Finland, which has one of the highest standards of education in the world, doesn't begin to teach its children formally until they're seven. Each school is autonomous, i.e. paid for by the state but not run by the state. Teachers are often more highly paid than doctors and must have Masters degrees. Teaching is a highly competitive profession and only about 10 per cent of those who apply to teach are accepted. At school, early childhood education is based on play, on nature, on learning to be in the physical environment. High-school students get fifteen minutes of one-on-one time with a teacher every week, which impacts their emotional lives significantly, especially when one compares it to the situation most teens face, which is often anonymity in a school environment with 2000 other teens and teachers who don't know individuals.[20]

In Finland, although children are tested informally when they're younger, they never see the results of those tests. Formal testing doesn't begin until they're fourteen, an idea that has now been adopted by Wales in the UK.

It's heartening that, in some places at least, awareness is growing that stressing children for the long term, with tests and measurable outcomes as part of their daily diet, actually *impedes* the development of intellectual capacity. Of course, this stress also gives rise to a physiological imbalance that later makes it more possible for disease to set in. It's distressing that in Australia, in the US and many parts of Europe and the UK as well as in most of the developing world, this fact isn't inspiring a global move towards educational reform in terms of reducing stress.

If we do measure anything, perhaps we should measure children's heart rhythms, discuss coherence ratios and the healthy function of the autonomic nervous system, and make sure that these are optimum.

We know that there are several billion ways of living our adult lives. We *know*, as adults who have been around a bit, that our high-school exams do not define us for life. So, surely we have to ask ourselves what the purpose is of these unwitting crimes we so often and so constantly commit against our children? They pay for it too often with their health, and sometimes with their lives.

Let's now take a look in more detail at those 'buffers' that help to stop teen stress from becoming unmanageable and that can counter the stressors that they may often have to face.

A functional family

A functional family is one where there is an absence of neglect and, of course, of physical and emotional abuse. In a functional family, conflict gets resolved more often than not and communication, affection and quality time are shared among family members. A functional family is one where every member feels accepted and has the space to be who they are.

Creating a functional family depends entirely on the way the adults in the family conduct themselves. How *we* respond to the stressors of raising children defines the functionality of the family dynamic. If we can be conscious of how we respond to the dramas of childhood right from the start, we can map a healthy road ahead for our children. The next time your eight-year-old drops the soda and spills it all over the floor, check your response. You could 1) react stressfully and point out what he already knows, that he's made a mess, and the guaranteed result will be guilt, a feeling of inadequacy and low self-esteem. And of course no insurance that he will never ever drop another soda bottle in his life. Or, you could 2) keep your voice even, say, 'Oops!' and show him where the paper towels are, even handing him a bunch to get started cleaning up. The second option, if that becomes your pattern of response, will lead to your child becoming a teenager who feels trusting enough that he can come to you the week after he gets his driver's licence and tell you that he backed your car into a new Mercedes. You might be distressed, but you won't imply that he's an idiot and you'll help him to find out how much needs to be paid, what's covered by insurance and how he can make reparation of some sort. You'll tell him you're glad it was only a minor accident and that he's okay. In this kind of functional family, the risk of your teen being depressed, feeling misunderstood or being over-whelmed by stress is going to be minimised because neither he nor you will have an over-reactive sympathetic nervous system.

My sixteen-year-old students explained to me that parents cause stress by a) expecting teens to take adult responsibility for certain things, like caring for younger siblings, making dinner, running errands and then b) treating them like small children — not trusting them, nagging them and criticising them. They are often living lives with as much adult responsibility as some parents, and yet they are being graded on their 'performance' and found lacking by critical parents.

'When I get home from school,' said one, 'I just want to be left alone. I'm tired, I need some down time and I want to go into my room and close my door. It's not because I don't love my parents, but I just need some space. I don't want to go into the details of how my day went and I don't want someone nagging me or telling me what needs to be done.' They expressed that stressors came from trying to find out who they were in relation to others. 'I'm stressed by family dynamics. I want to be a good daughter/friend/sister and sometimes it's pretty much impossible because of how others behave. It isn't always easy.'

So, as parents we can assume that to create a functional family, everyone needs respect, space and, importantly, time to be alone.

Friends

Friends give teens the emotional support that only people of the same generation can give one another. With a few real friends, teenagers can feel that they exist, that they are loved, that they are okay in the world. With peers who see a friend's unique value, teens have somewhere to turn when the going gets tough. They're all in the same teen boat trying to navigate the raging hormonal seas, and bonds are formed during this time that can be literal lifesavers when the adult world has forgotten what it feels like to be there. As parents, we can make both the physical and emotional space for our teens to feel that they can bring friends home. If we're concerned that our children might be 'getting up to no good' when they go out with their friends, a powerful response is to create an appealing space where our teens can 'hang out' and this might involve some effort from us. Social events don't have to be glamorous. Our teens want to be with each other and there's value in creating a supportive social environment that makes our children feel part of a functional community.

One of my friends recently had to tell her fifteen-year-old son that he couldn't go and hang out until late with his buddies in a rather seedy area of town, where she knew drugs and alcohol might be part of the picture. Instead she invited all of those same buddies to spend the whole day on a boat with her son and the rest of the family. The youngsters got to be together, which was what they really wanted, and the parent supported the friendships by creating a healthy context and minimising risk. It takes effort but it's so worth it in the end.

Recreation

Every 26,000 years or so, the earth's axis shifts enough so that what is now summer in the southern hemisphere, will, in so many years' time, be winter; and vice versa in the northern hemisphere. This is called 'precession'. Every day, the average human being takes an average of 26,000 breaths. And an average lifespan of around 72 years is approximately 26,000 days.

We're creatures who are inextricably linked to large rhythms beyond the earth. Everything in our solar system, including us, is tied to a certain rhythm set in motion many years before human consciousness was there to take note of it. Our hearts beat to a certain rhythm, we breathe to a certain rhythm; the earth and planets move to a specific rhythm around the sun. We forget we're in the solar system and that our pathway around the sun turns day to night, summer to winter, infants to adults. We forget that our breath is tied to the day, which is tied to the larger rhythms of the solar system. It's a big picture that gets lost in the business of everyday life. And in that rhythm, which is a kind of massive 'breathing', we need to remember that an out-breath is as important as an in-breath. Every day, we inhale and exhale approximately 26,000 times. When our teens sit and work and study and learn, we might see that as a metaphorical in-breath. The intense intellectual activity needs to be followed by an exhalation ... both literally and metaphorically. If you hear your teen sighing over a trigonometry question, you know what his body is trying to do.

Recreation, literally 're-creating', can be both metaphorically and physically an 'out-breath' an exhalation when we take time to go for a bike ride, a long walk or to have a game of table tennis. It's essential for physical and mental health. Teens can 're-create' autonomic nervous system balance when they're engaged in some form of recreation. The rhythm of breaking with 'head work' to do some kind of recreation creates a healthy rhythm that has immediate physical benefits, consequent emotional benefits and, as a result, supports better cognitive function and hopefully a lifespan that goes beyond 26,000 days.

Adventure

Teens, more than any other age group, have an innate need for adventure of some kind. Research has shown their brains respond very differently to the perception of threats or danger. From about age thirteen to seventeen, it takes a lot more to stimulate the 'reward' centre in their brains — and they are often spurred on to take risks, to do extreme things, in order to get the same sense of pleasure and achievement that came so easily when they were younger and that will return again when they're adults.

Every couple of years, my family and I travel to the UK to spend time with family. Since he was a toddler, my son always looked forward to the trip and anticipated it with growing excitement. This year he said sadly, 'I don't know what it is, but I'm just not excited anymore.' At the end of the holiday, he had had a wonderful time but said, 'Something's different. It didn't feel as exciting as it used to feel.'

I told him not to worry and that the sense of anticipation and excitement would return as he grew older, albeit in a different way.

As a teacher I often see students who were previously engaged and excited by life and their own achievements suddenly become careless and disengaged. Everything, apparently, is boring. I know that even if I taught standing on my head, I wouldn't eliminate the boredom factor.

But if adventure is part of their lives and teens have the opportunity to take on challenges that they set for themselves — particularly to do physically exhilarating things that challenge them, like climbing, abseiling, high-ropes courses, etc. — many of the other risk-taking behaviours that we so often see can be diminished. When I first started teaching at my current high school, we struggled with numerous discipline problems. The school had, to quote one parent, 'gone feral'. Slowly, though, with a lot of conversation, and the implementation of Restorative Practices, in which students are given the opportunity to repair and restore broken things and/or relationships before someone comes down hard in the punishment department, the entire mood has changed. I still deal with the odd group sneaking off into the bushes to have a smoke or climbing onto the roof, just for the thrill of doing something illicit. But in my experience, after our restorative conversations, those same people don't reoffend. Support them and support the need for adventure. I've directed students to do adventurous things in appropriate places. We have potential pilots, sailors and world travellers who have come back into the classroom after some adventures and been able to rekindle their interest in what academics have to offer.

As parents, we need the courage to sign up our teens for a sky dive or let them do the wild mountain biking they've been nagging about. Despite my terrible fear of flying, I've supported my son's gliding. I've even gone up myself, barely able to control my terror, to experience the world he loves. My own fear for him is very real but so is my desire to support his dream to fly. Of course there are risks involved, but tying our teens down and keeping them 'safe' is a risk in itself. They will find ways to get the thrills they need. And sometimes these are self-destructive. Allow them adventures in controlled risk environments. They need it and they'll feel much better for it.

Creativity

In a world where it's so easy to get things, and our needs and wants can be satisfied at the click of a button, many teens actually experience intense dissatisfaction and frustration.

What's often missing from their lives is the space to be genuinely creative in the deepest, broadest sense of the word. The world is in need of creative thinkers, and the place where this thing called 'creativity' resides is the imagination. When children are drawing or writing stories or composing music or acting, writing plays or designing a dream home, a whole element of self is invested in this act that has to do with *heart*.

Teens who have never had the opportunity to express themselves creatively as children often have a hard time accessing the source of creative endeavour, even though it resides in everyone. Creativity is innate. Imagination is a hungry, insatiable creature that lives in all of us, and each individual's imagination is as unique as a fingerprint. I've been teaching creative writing at schools and universities for twenty years and I've never seen the exact same story written twice. It always amazes me how endless and rich and constantly in action young people's imaginations are if you give them half a chance. Google and Microsoft and Facebook are the brainwaves of free-thinking and creative people who are unafraid to play. And yet, we brainwash our children into a kind of utilitarian, industrialised way of thinking so that eventually creativity is something that *other* people do, and those who have forgotten their own sources of inspiration simply consume the results of those other people's imaginations.

Movies are a prime example of this. They feed our imaginations — sometimes with the imaginative equivalent of carrot juice and wheatgrass, but sometimes with the equivalent of arsenic, which is why we have to be so discriminating about what we expose our children to. However, my point here is that the movie industry generates megabucks. From the earliest rock paintings to 3D television, the human race is deeply, uncompromisingly addicted to stories and narrative.

The same can be said about music. It feeds our 'soul' — the part of us that is engaged with the imaginative and emotional terrain of ourselves — and we spend fortunes every year on CDs, concerts and iTunes. Oliver Sacks, renowned neuroscientist and acclaimed writer of *Awakenings*, writes in his book *Musicophilia*: 'We humans are a musical species no less than a linguistic one … our auditory systems, our nervous systems, are indeed exquisitely tuned for music.'[21]

It's odd, but these very acts of creativity that are so innate, and for which we often pay and are paid handsomely, are often seen as non-essential to existence. I would argue that they are at the heart of what it means to be human. Look at where we put so much of our money! Politicians and presidents and CEOs and mining magnates will never be as revered or adored as the musicians, actors and even writers of the day. One of the richest people in the world is a writer who simply captured hearts and imaginations with her own. The 'Harry Potter' books all emerged from J.K. Rowling's head, and for years, children all around the globe in every language were devouring a single story made up by one woman.

I'm pretty sure that if we banned all forms of stories from the world and silenced music we'd soon die of depression and stress-induced diseases. I'm not advocating for such a trial, but in a way, when we cut arts programs in schools we're conducting a similar experiment — and we know that when we eliminate the arts (or, metaphorically, the heart) students at school do not fair better. In fact, they do a lot worse.

It's a fact that children are far happier in general when there's time to paint, to play music, or to build electric circuits and act things out. In a world without creativity, I, for one, would be in danger of losing the plot altogether. We have to feed our imaginations. Young children are the most vulnerable when we starve them of creativity and replace it with a diet of pure academics with a bit of sport thrown in for good measure. But teens suffer too when their diet is all head stuff and when there are not enough artistic or creative elements to balance it. The word 'poetry' means 'making'. Our artistic and creative impulses are related to joy and a deep sense of who we are and who we can become. Without the space to be creative, to make something ourselves, we take the 'heart' out of our lives. Our brains do not develop properly if we deprive them of the opportunity to build the extensive neural circuitry that results from playing music or engaging with the world creatively.

I'm surrounded by teens day and night, not just when I teach, but when I come home and there's a group of teens playing loud double bass and saxophone much to the neighbours' distress. It's important that they have the space to do that and that I, as a responsible parent, make sure that I don't tell them to cut it out but that I ask them to consider others, perhaps keep doors and windows shut, and end at an appropriate hour.

It seems to me that teens who have music as part of their daily diet have fewer issues with boredom and lassitude, and more energy to be creative in other areas of their lives. Being allowed to 'mess around' is an essential requirement for teens and enables their hearts to be 'fed' by doing things that engage them. Imagination and creativity are delicate creatures that are often squashed by parents and teachers as we strive to make teens conform and do things that we assume have a pragmatic purpose in their lives.

The benefits of allowing teens the tools and, more importantly, the space and the context at school and at home in which to be creative will have far-reaching positive emotional, physiological and cognitive impact. Sir Ken Robinson, knighted by the Queen for his dedicated advocacy for changing the way we educate children on a global scale, stated in a lecture entitled 'Schools Kill Creativity' that the current model of education was designed by academics as an echo of the university world they knew, primarily to meet the needs of industrialism. Ken Robinson says that we 'can't possibly afford to go on this way'. And further: 'My contention is that creativity now is as important in education as literacy and we should treat it with the same status ... I define creativity as the process of original ideas that have value.'[22]

As parents, we need to actively support and allow the space for this to happen.

Sleep

Sleep deprivation is anyone's nightmare. Those of us who have had sleepless babies know how we evolve into distorted monster-versions of our former selves when we're short of sleep. A recent experiment on the American show *Mythbusters* confirmed that a sleep-deprived adult is a far more dangerous driver than a tipsy one. For teens, however, sleep deprivation is a serious issue, compounded by physiological factors that impact their neurological development. It's not news that teens need nine to ten hours of sleep a night in order for them to function properly during the day, cognitively and emotionally. But it's not just that nine to ten hours is optimal; it's *essential* for healthy brain development.

Well-known research by a leading expert on teen sleep for well over a decade, Mary A. Carskadon, PhD, at the Bradley Hospital and Brown Medical School, New England, US, has shown that due to the hormonal changes teens experience, melatonin is released later during the day, making it very difficult for many of them to get to bed early. According to Carskadon, who tested the saliva of teens throughout the day and night, levels of melatonin begin to rise in teenagers on average between 10 and 11 p.m. — continuing until about 8 a.m. This late onset of melatonin secretion changes once people reach their twenties. Her research led to several school districts in the US changing the start-times for high schools, resulting in less depression among sleep-deprived teens. So, if their bodies are making it almost impossible for them to get to sleep early, and their schools are demanding them to be bright and ready to learn at 8 a.m., teens are caught between an unpleasant rock and an equally uninspiring hard place.[23]

And then there's the physiology of sleep and the important aspect of memory consolidation. In fact, whenever we learn something new, our brains 'practise' that process overnight, almost as if rehearsing it. While we sleep, our brains are actively merging, strengthening and combining all the elements of a new skill or series of ideas, so that when we wake up, a process, a skill, a new way of thinking has been consolidated.

There's a lot of truth in the saying 'sleep on it'. Sleep is essential for proper learning. If that sleep is disrupted, the learning process is impeded. Brain development is affected. In *NurtureShock*, Po Bronson and Ashley Merryman say that neurons lose plasticity with sleep deprivation, making them 'incapable of forming the new synaptic connections necessary to encode a memory'. The prefrontal cortex suffers the most and because it's responsible for 'executive function', i.e. the ability to fulfil a goal and come up with solutions, a child's capacity to learn is weakened, say Bronson and Merryman, who have noted importantly that our children get an hour less sleep than they did 30 years ago, and that the escalation of behaviour, obesity and learning issues can be largely attributed to this 'Lost Hour'.[24] But not only that. If youngsters spend 40 per cent of their sleeping time in slow-wave sleep (which they do, and which is ten times more than the average adult spends in slow-wave sleep), this impacts all learning and memory consolidation for the long term. And that's still not all. When we take note of teen depression, the lost hour of sleep and the fact that sleep deprivation leads to the brain processing emotions in such a way that negative memories are more easily accessed than positive ones, we're on the way to seeing how sleeping enough is as essential to our teens' wellbeing as food and water is to their physical survival. 'Negative stimuli get processed by the amygdala, positive or neutral memories get processed by the hippocampus,' say Bronson and Merryman. 'Sleep deprivation hits the hippocampus harder … sleep-deprived people fail to recall pleasant memories, yet recall gloomy memories just fine.'[25]

Sleep deprivation is a proven factor in increasing obesity, in learning disabilities and in problems with cognitive function. When children and teens lose sleep, as opposed to when adults do, there isn't such a thing as 'catch-up'. The effects are far-reaching. Remember, their brains are still vibrantly under construction and lack of sleep undermines that delicate process.

So, when that fourteen-year-old moves sluggishly through her breakfast routine and flings rude and monosyllabic words at us and is grumpy and upset with us for no apparent reason, we might try to remember what it felt like when she woke us every two hours to feed as a baby. We might remember how dysfunctional and upset we felt at 4 a.m. when every atom of ours was crying out for sleep and some torturer from a no doubt foreign planet was making impossible demands on us to pay attention and to be nice about it, too. If school begins too early and there's nothing we can do about our teen's lack of sleep, we could at least treat her with gentle, quiet understanding. It will minimise her stress … and everyone else's.

KEY POINTS

- Stress changes our physiology creating physical and psychological symptoms that can last a lifetime.

- Teens (and children) can be protected against stressors by having a functional family, friends, recreation and enough sleep.

- Those youngsters who have an exaggerated stress response need to be protected from stressors more than others.

- The biggest fallacy affecting our teens and children is that they have *one* shot at setting the course for the rest of their lives.

- Creativity is an absolute essential, as is enough sleep.

THE ACADEMIC PRESSURE COOKER

In the past 30 years, the suicide rate for young people aged 15 to 24 in Australia has more than tripled. After car accidents, it is the leading cause of death in this age group. And in the US, statistics show that since 2003 there's been a rapid increase in suicide among the 10 to 24-year-old age group.

Some research shows that more females than males attempt suicide, but that more males succeed, possibly because their methods are more violent and extreme.

In the US, research shows that academic pressure is a significant stressor on young people and that either a very poor academic record or one reflective of academic success can create unmanageable stress and lead to young people taking their own lives. A report by Henry, Stephenson, Hanson and Heirgett reveals that serious suicide attempts are often higher among students who experience considerable academic success. Less-serious suicide attempts are often more indicative of students who are failing at school, which might seem odd. These researchers, however, argued that academically successful students experience greater amounts of stress than do their less successful peers because more successful students feel more pressure to maintain high grades.

**This pressure may cause them to increase the
lethality of their suicidal intent. However, students
who have consistently exhibited a pattern of
academic failure may simply engage in risk-taking
behaviours (e.g. criminal acts, risky sexual activity)
that predispose them to suicidality.[26]**

If a child is overwhelmingly stressed by school, it seems important that while parents do their utmost to support their children, teachers also have a degree of creative autonomy and wherewithal to meet that need, using their own powers of critical thinking. As teachers, we know that one size does not fit all. And yet, if we devise different criteria for different children, not only do we run the risk of being accused of 'double standards' (or even 'multiple standards') but we would also kill ourselves with exhaustion trying to create programs specifically for each individual child. I do think, however, that there are creative ways of dealing with children who are stressed by schoolwork and the expectations we have of them, which could make or break someone who is 'on the edge'.

I share this story as a teacher, but its value for parents lies in the fact that we all carry the burden of placing (sometimes unrealistic) expectations on our young people, without seeing where their value and talents actually lie. If parents understand that a child is not actually going to be one of a small few who want to be serious academics, they might have discussions with all concerned parties about minimising stress and maximising learning of the relevant and inspiring kind. I know that this requires teachers to be just a little bit open and flexible, so if you find yourself in a school where this isn't the case, I'd move my child somewhere else, where it is.

Sean was in my Year 7 class a few years ago in Australia. Early in the year, he gave up on school. He decided that homework was not for him and he stopped doing it. His mother was in despair. She'd tried the whole menu — encouragement, punishment, cajoling, even bribery — and in the meantime Sean was, according to school rules, spending lunch times in detention doing homework, and driving every adult to distraction. His motivation was zero. He was failing everything. He'd started the school year as a sweet energetic boy with a great sense of humour but became increasingly rude, badly behaved and sullen. Most of his teachers wished quietly that he would just evaporate.

There were 28 children in the class and it took me a while to find out that Sean was on a rapid downward spiral to nowhere good. He wasn't coping at all with school, and his teachers weren't coping with his behaviour. I could see he worked slower than others. He had a mild learning disability for which he'd received help, but he was quite intelligent. So, I did something instinctive. This took, at most, fifteen minutes out of my day. I had a short meeting with Sean and asked him what the problem really was. At first he didn't know. Then he said school was boring. I asked him to explain that in more detail.

'If I don't do the work, I start to fall behind. Then I can't catch up and so I stop caring about anything,' he finally said. 'I don't give a stuff. It's boring.'

'Fine,' I said. 'Let's be creative about this. Are there any subjects you enjoy?'

'Probably only Manual Arts,' he said.

'What if you were given a special time slot, say, once a week and possibly during lunch times, to work on an individual project in manual arts?'

'That'd be cool,' he said.

I saw something like relief and gratitude on his face that was quite moving. Suddenly he saw that *I saw* that homework (or lack of it) was not a life-or-death situation, and that I wasn't viewing him as a future societal failure, but nor was I letting him off the hook in terms of task completion.

'Do you have any idea what you'd do?'

'I've got the plans in my head for a skateboard ramp,' he said. 'Could I do that?'

I said I'd arrange it with the Manual Arts teacher. Then I made a deal with him. I said that for the rest of the term I did not require any home-work from him in any of the subjects I taught. At that stage I had him for English, Maths and Geography. If he did the class work and came to me straight away with any problems, I would be right there for him to help find a solution. His side of the deal was that he would go during lunch and during one assigned period a week to the Manual Arts room and work on the project. We set a completion date for the end of term.

I organised Sean's times with the Manual Arts teacher, explaining that I felt it was really important for the future emotional and academic health of this student, and the teacher was supportive. I didn't speak to the rest of the class about Sean's 'special' treatment. Only one girl asked why he got to leave the class once a week and go to Manual Arts. 'I have an agreement with Sean and he's working on his side of it,' I said. She left it at that.

Sean did all his class work and no homework. At the end of the term, he arrived early on the morning of the last day of school, carrying some-thing bigger than he was. He plonked it down in front of the classroom door and his face glowed with satisfaction.

I came out and examined it carefully. It was a work of art: a skate-board ramp made out of wood and masonite, immaculately constructed and flawlessly finished. I admired his design, impressed by the way he'd created the supports and put it all together.

'This is the second one,' he said. 'I finished the first one last week and tried it out, but it totally broke. I had to make a much stronger frame. I nearly ran out of time, so I had to take it home. I spent pretty much all night on it last night. I just finished it and tried it today.'

'It looks like it survived,' I said.

'Do you think I could set it up on the basketball court on the day of the school fair?' he asked.

'Great idea,' I said. 'I'll find out how we can make that happen.' I added that I was really impressed with his hard work, his creativity and his dedication, especially after his first attempt. I shook his hand and this rebellious troublemaker grinned from ear to ear like a round-faced cherub.

He got to set it up at the fair and it survived use by dozens of admiring teens that day, much to his satisfaction.

From then on, Sean did every bit of work that I, and his other teachers, required. I was also more careful when handing out assignments. I gave out work that I thought was essential and meaningful. I questioned deeply what we are trying to achieve when we hand out homework to students who already spend most of their waking hours at school.

I think it is simply this: we know that as adults we need to be self-motivated. We understand that a healthy work ethic is essential in the modern world. We therefore think that when children are doing homework, they are being trained to 'work on their own' to 'do things in their own time' and so we are giving them practice at being good grown-ups with the capacity to work hard.

Again, I believe to a large extent, that we create the very problem we seek to avoid: as teachers, we often demotivate our students because they are mentally exhausted and stressed, because often the homework is repetitive headwork, just more of the same, and not engaging their hearts, the place from which true motivation comes. Once Sean's heart was engaged in a project, he had no issues with 'motivation' or working late into the night to complete something and to complete it well. He was on the knife-edge when I proposed his project. He was one warning short of being suspended. I know he absolutely doubted his ability to be successful in the world. After the project, he knew that he could do anything he wanted to do … if his heart was in it. And that was enough to change everything and to give him the confidence and energy to tackle other tasks that were less appealing, something we know we have to do in the world as adults.

KEY POINTS

- Stressed teens can dissolve quickly into demotivated teens.

- Listening to what the problem *really* is, is part of the solution.

- Schools are heavily academically one-sided and, given this reality, a good percentage of teens need teachers and parents to respond to them creatively.

- Youngsters need to feel that their parents (and ideally their teachers) value their unique qualities.

- Adding a single joyful motivator can lift a young person out of the doldrums.

THE PHYSICAL
ENVIRONMENT

The way we are and the way we respond to the children in our lives profoundly affects their wellbeing. Their environments and the rhythms of their days also impact their health.

This includes the physical environment. Just as a foetus needs the ideal environment of the womb to survive, children at different stages of their development need different types of physical environments in order to thrive. The immediate environment is critical for survival when a baby is in utero but the environments surrounding our children as they grow still play a critical role in forming who our children become physiologically, socially and intellectually.

We gradually grow blind to the fact that the homes and classrooms that our children inhabit for most of their waking hours play a significant role in their development.

A few years ago when we were living in the US state of Oregon, I taught Adult Education and GED (high-school diploma) skills to inmates at the Eastern Oregon Correctional Institute. This building had once been a mental hospital and was the inspiration for Ken Kesey's *One Flew Over the Cuckoo's Nest*.

The corridors were squeaky clean. Metal and tiles and fluorescent lights lined the walk from the three massive security doors that slid or clanged shut behind me, up the elevator, to the education department. The inmates' 'uniform' was blue jeans and blue denim shirts. Officers patrolled the corridors sporadically with loaded revolvers on their hip belts. Everything was quiet and calm and eerily 'normal'. This place was a far cry from Leeuwkop Prison in South Africa, where I once went as a teen with a drama group to perform a Christmas play some years before the end of apartheid. A filthy, crowded mass of humanity was held in a few brick buildings. In that South African prison at the height of apartheid, I walked, unbelieving, past tiny cells crammed with inmates, who were dangling their arms out between the bars of their cells like animals in cages. The scene was every bit as heart-stopping as the movies make such things out to be. Executions were still taking place every month, at that very place, by hanging.

So, when I went to teach at the prison in Oregon, or, should I say, the 'Correctional Institute', I was, at first, desperately relieved to see that human beings, whatever their crimes, were not being kept in conditions unfit for any living things on earth. I thought then that it was better. And perhaps, in a sense, it was. And yet, there was still the perpetual threat of violence or death throughout every moment of every day. A riot could break out (which sometimes happened), resulting in a lockdown. Someone could escape (which he did, through a chapel window using sheets stolen from the laundry), resulting in a manhunt. No human being wants to be kept locked up, stripped of dignity and self in any kind of environment, under threat. This prison was a medium-security facility and the inmates' sentences ranged from five years to life. Crimes ranged from theft and drug offences to murder.

Environments can actively mitigate against a human being finding his way to anything redemptive, restorative or healing. I imagine the corridors on Death Row are equally clean and well lit, but I'm not convinced we can say that good things have come of that. One of the worst crimes we commit against our fellow human beings is the crime of dehumanisation. It leads to people murdering each other. We call innocent human beings who die in civil war 'civilian casualties' or 'collateral damage'. The human being doesn't feature here.

Whether a prison is a filthy rat's hole in the middle of Africa or a sterile steel-and-tile corridor filled with armed guards, the people in these places have been stripped of their humanity. Once we do that, we can be sure that these people will have a near-impossible task to rehabilitate or re-integrate *healthily* into society.

I have taught murderers and arsonists and kidnappers and drug dealers and gang-leaders how to read and spell and understand algebra. The only 100 per cent effective program to prevent recidivism was one conducted by a psychiatrist who directed the Massachusetts Prison Mental Health Service; it allowed inmates to receive a college degree while they were in prison. 'Several hundred prisoners in Massachusetts had completed at least a bachelor's degree while in prison over a 25-year period, and not one of them had been returned to prison for a new crime.'[27]

That's pretty staggering. I've seen young men who imagined their futures as bleak dark tunnels ending in some unmarked urban grave burn with the desire to turn their lives around, given half a chance. All it takes sometimes is another human being's interest and concern, acknowledgement of his humanity, and a 21-year-old drug dealer who would have surely been shot dead before long has decided to use his five years in prison to plan a youth venture to keep other at-risk youngsters off the street and out of trouble.

If this young man had not found himself selected because of good behaviour to participate in the education program in that prison, he would have been another number, a nameless prisoner, a threat to society, one of nearly 2000 inmates wearing blue jeans and a shirt, confined to a cell.

Most ordinary citizens don't get to see the insides of prisons. If they did they might be surprised. My shock deepened when, while I taught at the prison, I also had the opportunity to run writers' workshops at the local high school. At first, walking down the corridors of the school past all the classrooms, my thoughts were, well, that prison's really not so bad, it's just like the high school.

And then I thought: maybe that's a very bad thing indeed. It's not that the *prison's* a lot like the school, it's that the school is, oh horror, a lot like the prison. Okay, so instead of officers, we have teachers 'patrolling' the corridors. But the design of this particular school, and many other state schools across the world (the US, the UK, Australia and South Africa), is very similar. It's all concrete and steel — austere and functional, designed to be 'secure' and economical. Many of the government architects who design these buildings are also the designers of state penitentiaries. Here's a note from a Facebook page called 'Schools look like prisons'.

> **When I come to school, I always notice how colourless and boring the school is, similar to a prison. Plus during school hours we are all locked up inside, and almost nobody goes in or out. Take away some decor, and you got a prison![28]**

Our children begin their lives supported by a lovingly and carefully chosen environment. How we decorate a new baby's bedroom, the colours and themes and furniture — everything we put in there is selected based on our understanding and imagination of what our little ones will need surrounding them in order to make them feel loved and happy. It's odd then that a few short years later it's okay to stick them in harshly lit boxes for seven hours a day. It's suddenly fine that we line them up, even when they're four or five, and dish out punishments and rewards, treating them as a herd that needs to conform; we often have uniforms for convenience or to support the idea that everyone's equal.

In these concrete-and-steel boxes, it's often the case that we treat the next generation as potential wrongdoers. We imperceptibly, and inadvertently, divest them of individuality and treat them as a mass that needs to be kept under control.

My son started Kindergarten at a public school in Oregon and on his second day my husband went to fetch him. My son was five. There was the teacher, herding 40 kindergartners out of a solid, square concrete building and yelling at them to keep in line as they wandered, dazed, into the afternoon air. The teacher yelled out my son's name with such vehemence he thought he was being punished. He shook and stuttered with fright. But she was only trying to tell him his father was there. My husband lifted my son over the wire fence, the very same wire fence used to keep prisoners separate from decent society (except this fence was without the electric barbed wire on top).

When he got home my husband said, 'We just can't send him there. It's like the army.' And he would know. He'd been conscripted to fight in a war in Zimbabwe as an eighteen-year-old and lost half his class and nearly lost his life. He knew the psychology of turning individuals into units and platoons. Basic training was all about being yelled at and pushed into lines. This was supposed to be Kindergarten, not a military precursor for under-sevens.

Without knowing it, the very architecture, both physically and metaphorically, of our schools is often a far-too-close echo of prison. This construct lends itself, not to individuals developing to their fullest potential, but to individuals being crushed into a conforming mass, an economic work force, a platoon, which will defend a country. It lends itself to individuals being vulnerable to becoming treated as a prison population.

Physical environment and the ensuing emotional response to it is a significant part of the problem that leads so many children to feel that they are worthless and invisible.

Environment isn't everything. But it's a lot more important than we might imagine.

It's much harder to generate a coherent heart rhythm pattern in a stressful and 'cold' environment. Strangely, though, as a society, we think that being in stressful, even ugly schools and workplaces is the norm, and that during holidays we go somewhere beautiful to relax and 'get away from it all'.

It's really no wonder that children often feel and say that school is like prison. They don't know this from experience, but they're absolutely right. The architects who design school buildings are mostly utilitarian. Aesthetics don't come high on the list unless it's a private school and that school wants to attract 'customers'.

If we designed schools with children's development and wellbeing at heart, they would look absolutely *nothing at all* like prisons.

If you live in a metal cell with a sink and a hole in the floor for a toilet, in the name of public security, your mental health is not going to improve by being there. And so, if a child spends most of his waking hours in a school environment, it's really important to look at the physical and aesthetic details of that environment.

When we choose schools for our children, we have quite a bit of freedom. We most often think of schools with the best 'reputation', or good teachers, or excellent academic results, all of which are important. But as we look at our children and notice the phase they are in, it makes sense to look at the architecture and layout of the place where they will be spending so much of their time.

Depending on a child's age, our questions before enrolling our children in school might look like this: if it is a preschool, is it set out in a way that is similar to a home environment? Our child is maybe three or four, and needs to be somewhere where there is still a degree of softness, gentle colours, small corners and play areas. The child also needs an outdoor area for play. And then, remembering how little bodies need to move, there should be logs and climbing equipment and swings, and as much as possible that supports physical movement.

If our child is starting primary school, the next gentle step away from the ideal preschool environment is a classroom that is cheerful, warm and not an ADHD recipe, with TVs blaring and a million posters on the wall. Most importantly, though, there still needs to be an outside area for playing and climbing, and the timetable should include ample time to enjoy those outdoor activities. Remember that sound neurological development is inextricably connected to healthy physiological and emotional development.

By the time middle and high school arrive, we seem to forget about the aesthetics of environment all together. Some of the ugliest, most depressing buildings I have seen are high-school buildings. In Sarasota, Florida, the local high school was half a block away from our house. During the four years we lived there, the school paved their several acres of green to make a car park for hundreds of students. The classrooms were a series of grey and orange concrete Lego blocks, with a series of portable/demountable boxes humming with air-conditioners. I would be seriously depressed if someone committed me to that environment and expected me to be happy and learn.

Recently, in Australia, as we drove up the east coast through a town near Rainbow Beach, a major tourist destination, the building I thought was surely the closest thing to a prison I had ever seen was, in fact, the local high school. It was grey and drab and fenced in, as if its primary purpose was to keep people in. Of course I'm not saying that there aren't great teachers or good things happening in these places, or that they aren't supported with fantastic equipment, etc. But these buildings are housing our *children*. These individuals who are still growing and forming all their opinions, whose emotional lives are delicately under construction, who have committed no crimes, who need to be loved for who they are individually, are sitting for seven hours a day inside rooms and buildings that look about as uplifting as a medium-security prison's education department.

And then we wonder that some of them just want to die.

High-school students need a school environment that is *aesthetically pleasing* and that has places where they can socialise during breaks. We can't put them in a tile-and-concrete environment and expect them to be overjoyed. They need areas where they can just relax and 'hang out', which is what they should be doing to develop properly. The architecture of an environment has far-reaching social and emotional consequences and can either enhance and facilitate certain behaviours or prevent them. There's been extensive research on the effects of architecture and community, but it doesn't take a degree in psychology to figure out that places with inviting central areas and places to sit support socialisation, while others prevent it.

An environment that says 'here's a place for you', whether that's a special lounge room or a picnic table under a tree or the equivalent of a student union, allows young people to feel that they and their needs matter. At the huge public school a few minutes from my house in Sunshine Beach, Queensland, even though the buildings are square and not overly attractive, there are enough grassy, shady areas and sheltered tables for everyone, and a senior lounge where older students can work. The library is open to them all at any time and the principal has just implemented a program of Restorative Practice, so that before anyone gets to the punishment stage, regardless of the 'crime', students are given an opportunity to repair and restore broken things and/or relationships. That school is nothing fancy, but it's a far cry from anything resembling a prison.

One of many architects in Australia is responsible for extensive government projects. Employed by a state-funded 'School's Group' to design buildings for the department of education, he designed schools (of course) and early-childhood centres, but also a major state prison and a police academy. He's probably a really nice guy, and very smart and good at what he does in a fundamentally utilitarian way. My point, though, is that if these people who design prisons also design schools, then the same ethos prevails — buildings are cost-effective, utilitarian, secure — as opposed to the focus of an architect who might be designing a school as an ideal learning facility with aesthetically pleasing elements and high functionality that, above all, supports emotional and psychological wellbeing.

Our hearts are responding to our environment with every breath that we take. If we're happy in a certain space, we won't feel stressed. Our bodies will be healthier and our brains will consequently be in better condition to do the work we need them to do.

The schools where we send our children shouldn't just be functional and secure. They should support our children as they develop from tots to teens in a way that is appropriate for each stage of their development. And as we decide on the educational environments that our children will be inhabiting for six or seven hours a day, we might cast more than just a cursory glance over the actual facility, and see what we feel in that space, before we make any kind of commitment in the name of our children.

KEY POINTS

- The physical environment surrounding our children affects them.

- Buildings that look like prisons result in students who feel like they're in prisons.

- Aesthetics have social and psychological repercussions.

- Schools with inviting central areas and places to sit facilitate healthy socialisation.

- Choose schools carefully since children spend many hours a day in this environment.

VIRTUAL REALITY

In the past few years, computer games were given a bad rap by researchers in terms of a) their effects on children's behaviour — an increase in violent behaviour and desensitisation to violence occurs, and b) the amount of time children spend *not* engaging properly in physical activity, with the resulting lack of physiological and neurological benefits that come with moving their bodies.

Then several reports began to circulate in the media claiming that the ideas behind the games were often educational and even beneficial to social and cognitive development, and that games therefore warranted a more balanced and forgiving approach. After all, who can argue that a game based on keeping a family alive and planting vegetables, looking after pets, etc. could be in any way damaging? Those with negative bias towards computer games were accused of fear mongering, the argument being that every time new technology is introduced a wave of unwarranted fear ripples across the world, just as it did with the introduction of television.

But maybe our fears originate in a real concern that we often blindly go about damaging our society, our children in particular, in subtle and long-lasting ways, discovering the negative long-term effects only when it's too late.

Children spend an inordinate amount of time in front of various screens. After 50 years of research on the effects of television, a groundbreaking article entitled 'The Violent Face of Television' consolidated the findings of several decades' worth of research.[29] Though arguments and debates about television and the effects on young children still abound, the facts are out there: there is a distinct correlation between violence on television and violent and antisocial behaviour in children, teens and adults. Even cartoons with violence are part of the equation.

Young children, for whom one of the primary ways of learning is by imitation, emulate what they see. The mesmerising quality of the screen impacts teens and adults too.

A recent shooting in a cinema in the US town of Aurora, Colorado, where the killer dressed up as one of the characters in the movie being shown and then proceeded to gun down members of the audience, has drawn widespread discussion, first from people claiming that this kind of violence was the random act of a madman and then from those claiming that the creators of violent films are directly responsible for inspiring violent behaviour. In an online article on *The Daily Beast*, writer Blake Gopnik says, 'If you're going to lose control anyway, they [movies] provide a model for how to go about it.'[30]

But as we've seen, after 50 years of television, the evidence is in: there *is an undeniable parallel* between violence on screen and violent behaviour. We don't just get the *model* for how to carry out violent acts. We are psychologically and physiologically deeply affected by what we watch, and our nervous systems respond to what we see in a very similar way to how they would respond if we were participating in the actual event ourselves.

A diet of screen violence influences neural patterning and affects our stress responses to the world. Young children are at high risk because they don't possess the cognitive ability to make the distinction between *their* reality and the screen reality.

Many parents feel that they do guard against their children watching violence or playing violent screen games. But, compounding the issue is the actual medium itself and how it functions. Even in the most peaceful documentary, images are changing with untold rapidity, giving rise to a generation with an attention span that mirrors those rapidly changing images.

Viewing *any* kind of screen, whether it's a high-definition television or a seemingly innocuous game on an iPad, measurably impacts children. Dr Mary Burke, Associate Clinical Professor of Child and Adolescent Psychiatry at the University of San Francisco writes, 'In essence, screen media constitute neurologically potent, arousing input to the developing brain. Unlike conventional toxins, their effects are mediated by sense organs. However, they have demonstrable effects on brain activity visualized on functional MRI (fMRI) and on behaviour and function.'

She found that youngsters who spent more than twenty hours a week playing computer games, regardless of the type of game, showed increased glucose metabolism in certain parts of the brain, and decreased metabolism in other parts of the brain, after playing. 'These patterns were similar to those seen in drug addicts,' she writes. Now there's a sobering thought.[31]

Engagement with media of any kind impacts behaviour, and even though there are often negative consequences (Burke cites texting while driving and the resultant increase in accidents), young people most often cannot give up their addictions. Having screens at home means we have to be extraordinarily vigilant as parents. The way media affects the brain goes beyond addiction. It impacts the way our children learn and consolidate memories during sleep.

When we sleep, something incredible happens that is worth remembering: all-important consolidation of skills happens. This takes place primarily during slow-wave sleep (SWS). It's as if the brain rehearses new things learned and consolidates that learning. But what happens in our children's brains after hours of watching television or playing computer games is quite alarming.

Firstly, children who play computer games (of any kind) show a disruption in slow-wave sleep. They actually spend less time in slow-wave sleep, which then impacts the prefrontal cortex and results in impeded learning capacity and memory. Children who watch television have reduced sleep efficiency, according to research done at the Institute of Motor Control and Movement Technique at German Sport University in Cologne:[32]

> **Excessive television viewing and computer game playing have been associated with many psychiatric symptoms, especially emotional and behavioural symptoms, somatic complaints, attention problems such as hyperactivity, and family interaction problems.**

They acknowledged that there was, up until that point:

> **... insufficient knowledge about the relationship between singular excessive media consumption on sleep patterns and linked implications on children. The aim of this study was to investigate the effects of singular excessive television and computer game consumption on sleep patterns and memory performance of children.**

And they discovered:

The results suggest that television and computer game exposure affect children's sleep and deteriorate verbal cognitive performance, which supports the hypothesis of the negative influence of media consumption on children's sleep, learning, and memory.

From what we already know about the importance of enough good-quality sleep in terms of learning and brain development, this is essential information. And of course, children's brains are being formed every second of the day, so what they do repeatedly matters enormously.

Media affects children's stress response. In fact, any kind of media can become an acute stressor. In one experiment, fMRIs (functional Magnetic Resonance Imaging) were used to show brain activity in children playing an exciting Nintendo game compared with a group of children doing the seemingly mundane task of adding single-digit numbers.

In the Nintendo group, only the visual cortex lit up, and very little other activity was shown. For the other group, the left and right brain showed activity, indicating creative and logical processes were being engaged.

Further research using fMRIs shows that the neurological effects on children watching TV programs — even cartoons — with violent events are the same as if children actually experienced violent and traumatic events. And the areas affected in the brain correspond with behaviours that are indicative of post-traumatic stress disorder, or PTSD.

If we consider the themes inherent in most computer games (you're either pursuing something or someone in order to destroy them, or you are being pursued and have to escape), it's not hard to see that, even though the game is virtual, the effect on the physiology of the game-player would be absolutely real. But what if, as the argument sometimes goes with parents who can't see the problem with media, our child's online game looks cute and benign and all she has to do is feed a cyber-pet? Surely that's okay? After all, it's teaching her to take care of something and be responsible. Well, let's not forget about the pressure here. If she doesn't feed that cyber-pet, it 'dies' — and she will experience not virtual trauma but real trauma in her developing brain.

It's all fight-or-flight. These games are the ultimate sympathetic nervous system stimulus. We've just imported an instant stress machine into our midst. And the tragedy is that as our children disappear into a cyber-world of vast dimensions we have no idea what their nervous systems are doing and how their brains are being affected because we're not watching their brains on an fMRI, we can't see their heart rhythms, and they're not being tested after playing for memory consolidation and glucose levels in the brain.

Studies show that children's central nervous systems are impacted continuously during the playing of computer games: heart rates increase and there are surges of dopamine and adrenaline.

Remember that our children's brainwaves can entrain to their heart's rhythms. Harmonious ordered patterns in heart rhythms result in harmonious ordered brainwave patterns. It's easy to see then that while our children are engaged in some quiet battle on a computer game or television show, even when these shows are cartoons, their accelerated heart rates are not at the centre of a coherent heart-rhythm pattern. This is going to have a marked effect on their brainwave patterns and, over time, on their neurological make-up.

After 50 years of research, we know *definitively* that the results are anything but desirable.

So, as our child sits quietly in front of a screen, behaving himself and thankfully not causing any trouble, his heart might be racing and his body is potentially flooded with stress hormones. He is glued to the screen in what is often a virtual life-or-death battle with real physiological consequences.

Add to this the fact that he's not getting up and using all the glucose that has been released to get to the haven of a 'safe verandah'. His limbs are inert as blood pounds through his system, as adrenaline circulates and as his heart races in response to images that have no basis in the real world.

The result, among many other things, can be an over-active sympathetic nervous system — a propensity to fall into the fight-or-flight mode at any opportunity. And we know that behavioural disorders correlate directly with over-active sympathetic nervous systems.

Violent cartoons, computer games and television shows result in aggressive, antisocial behaviour in children and in adults. They result in those children and adults being much more likely to try to solve social conflict with aggression and violence. They result in desensitisation to violence and 'Mean World Syndrome', a prevalent, fearful response to the world.[33]

In our busy lives as parents, this is disconcerting and inconvenient information, but it's information we've got to take note of and acknowledge, whether we like it or not. Violence is the ultimate stress crime, against others, and sometimes, against ourselves. Over the past 50 years, research has confirmed that violence on television impacts viewer behaviour, resulting in aggression, desensitisation and fear.[34]

In fMRIs used to detect responses in children to violence on the screen, children viewing violent TV show activity in brain areas involved in arousal and attention, threat detection and long-term memory storage of the threat event (similar to the patterns seen in post-traumatic stress disorder — PTSD — patients). The right hemisphere and some bilateral areas are selectively affected by watching violent television, suggesting that there is significant emotional processing going on during this viewing. This contrasts dramatically with the brains of children *not* watching violence, where these areas are not activated at all. We still need to keep in mind, though, that the mere act of watching television (violent or not) impacts quality of sleep.[35]

So, if we take the escalating test and exam stress, combine it with the modern things we think of as 'down time' for our children (movies, television, a new DS game, social networking — which comes with a whole new panorama of stresses of its own), and add that to our own family stresses and our responses that so often fall short of our ideal, is it any wonder that our teenagers engage in destructive and self-destructive behaviour?

As parents, we need to be the moderators. We need to have control. Media is out there. We need to protect our youngest children from it and actively engage our older children in discussions and even workshops about it so that they are empowered viewers and participants with the ability to discern the good from the bad. We can't run the risk of being negligent or indulgent, or thinking that this is so much part of our world that it can't do any harm.

Consider this: if our young children do not watch any television or play a single computer game, they will not experience any kind of social, emotional or cognitive deficit. But if they are exposed to even quite small amounts, the risk of them being affected is very high indeed. As they grow older, if they learn about how films and computer games are constructed, and if they become critics and viewers who are able to deconstruct the images that pour into their lives, who are able to understand and discuss the motivations of the movie makers and game makers, they will be much better protected against the negative impact of television and computer games, and the negative impact of these mediums will be lessened enormously.

At the New York International Fringe Festival in 2011, a new play premiered. Sarah B. Weir, who runs a parenting blog, interviewed some of the young cast, who spoke about their relationship to social networking.[36] (The teens' names have been changed.)

> 'There's more "life" happening online than offline. If you are not online, you are completely out of the loop — you don't have a life, you don't really exist.'
> — *Hannah, thirteen years old*

> 'I'm online even during class. I'm supposed to be taking notes but instead I'm commenting on stuff and uploading pictures.' — *Emma, fourteen years old*

> 'I feel safer online than I do offline. So I do things online that I wouldn't do in real life.' — *Sasha, fourteen years old*

> 'I've become very good at taking pictures of myself. I know what angle is best, I know how to part my lips ... you know. It's like the number one thing on my mind is "I need to get home right now and take a new profile picture." All because I want someone to comment on how I look.' — *Katie, fifteen years old*

> 'Social networking affects all the things you do in real life now. Like, if you go to a party, one of the most important aspects of going to the party is to document yourself for online posts. You have to prove you were looking good, you were having fun, and that you were actually there! It's not about the party anymore but about the pictures of the party.'
> — *Caroline, fourteen years old*

**'I feel sad, depressed, jealous, or whatever when
I don't get a lot of "Likes" on my photo or when
someone else gets way more Likes than me.
Honestly, I'm not sure that parents realise how
drastically it affects our self-image and confidence.
If I see a picture of a really pretty girl, it's like
"Goodbye self-esteem." It forces me to compete and
do stuff that I don't want to do, so my confidence will
get a boost.'** — *Samantha, fourteen years old*

**'Sometimes I feel like I'm losing control. I want my
parents to tell me to get off the computer. Actually,
they would need to literally take the computer away
because I can't stop myself.'** — *Nina, fifteen years old*

**'My friendships are really affected by social
networking. You have to constantly validate your
friends online. And everyone's like "Where were
you?" "What have you been doing?" "Why haven't
you commented on my picture yet?" So you have to
be online all the time, just to keep track, so you don't
upset anyone.'** — *Jasmine, thirteen years old*

The stresses inherent here are obvious. The teens are constantly being hassled to be 'on' — and the lack of parental control or guidance is obvious. To have a child actively wishing her parents would take her away from this media nightmare should be enough of a wake-up call for any parent.

Recently, I was teaching a literature class on the mediaeval tome *Parzival*, by Wolfram von Eschenbach. As an exercise in self-discipline, I asked the class of sixteen- and seventeen-year-olds to select 'knightly' tasks that required some kind of staying power for the several weeks of class. They could commit to physical exercise, to giving up chocolate, to being more understanding of younger siblings, and so on. One student decided to give up Facebook for three weeks. After week one she said, 'I'm horrified. I keep getting notified by Facebook that things are happening on it while I've been away. It's designed to actually make you feel stressed, as though life is moving on without you. I'm actually quite stressed about it. I feel awful.' We went on to have a discussion. The class identified that the powers behind Facebook were using the vulnerabilities of teens to create a tight net in which they were caught.

As parents, we have to facilitate critical thinking in our teens and have open, interested and interesting discussions if we don't want them to fall victim to yet more media stress that, as evidenced by the comments of American teens, has the power to create untold anxiety in a cyber-world of pseudo-socialising.

For a realistic and humorous account of what happens when a family gives up every electronic and 'necessary' communication tool, every device in their household for six months, Susan Maushart's book *The Winter of Our Disconnect* provides a thought-provoking account of how *disconnecting* from all this media led one family to actually *re-connect* with each other.

There are some very practical and straightforward approaches to the problems created by screens and technology. Small children don't need 'screen time' at all, so I'd limit exposure to the absolute minimum without ever making a fuss. Once children start school, I'd keep all screen time very limited, a few hours a week at most. As children get older, I'd engage in interested and interesting conversations about the technology behind what we see or watch, so that by the time children reach a more independent age, they understand as much as we do, why we have to be vigilant and protect ourselves against being sucked into the cyber-vortex.

I tell all my teens that technology is there to be our slave and to assist us, not the other way around. If we find ourselves 'enslaved' to a game or a program or things like Facebook, we need to be conscious enough to rescue ourselves.

KEY POINTS

- There is a direct link between violence on TV and violent or fearful/antisocial behaviour in children.

- Watching TV compromises the quality of sleep, regardless of the program.

- Playing games on-screen disrupts and shortens slow-wave sleep resulting in an impeded learning capacity and memory.

- Computer games impact children's nervous systems: heart rates increase and there are surges of dopamine and adrenaline.

- Aside from the anti-social aspect of screen time, children and teens become physically addicted to viewing/playing.

SUPPORTIVE EMOTIONAL ENVIRONMENTS

At the beginning of the book, I examined the effect of the parent's emotional state on the child. The emotional environment that we, as parents, create affects our growing children more significantly than all other environments. From birth until our children leave home, they will be formed by the reality we create. Here are some practical suggestions for how we might go about creating emotional environments that support our children during each phase of development.

Birth to six

We parents are the primary element of our children's emotional and psychological environment. What we do and how we respond to our children creates the home environment. We are the adults in the situation, so from the very beginning of our children's lives *we* set the tone and create what will either be a happy and loving or stressful environment.

The minute we're aware that our behaviour and our emotions impact our children's nervous systems and create the neural patterning in our children's brains, we can start looking at our parenting style and begin to adopt strategies and responses that minimise stress and maximise love, joy and connection. It's also worth being acutely aware of exactly what's going on physically at each stage of development, so that we can do the right thing at the right time.

When my son was three weeks old, we left South Africa and went to teach in the Middle East. I definitely don't recommend this as the ideal start to a new life as a family. Those first two years of my child's life in an apartment in virtual isolation staring out at the dusty desert while the outside temperature rocketed to 57 degrees Celsius were an exercise in survival. I think post-partum depression is too mild a term for all that. Only the fact that I was crucial to the survival of my tiny precious (and very sleepless) baby stopped me from wanting to leap off the balcony into wild traffic. I did, though, fantasise day and night about how to escape. If pregnancy was hard in South Africa, having a baby and then a toddler in the Middle East, far away from friends, family and support, took the cake. Stress I have known!

At some deep level, we know that our babies need us to be loving and to fill their young lives with joy. I found a way to do this in my Arabian Desert years. I saw the world through my toddler's eyes and treasured the newness of everything. The very few leaves, the moon, the water, even the rubbish truck and the gas truck were things of wonder. I rediscovered the world. In a fairly unappealing space, we found joy. I think to a large degree, that sense of wonder dissolved much of the stress and exhaustion of being a young mother in a pretty desolate situation. Every response of ours is written into our children. They learn from us how to be.

So, when our toddlers do things that are 'naughty', what do we do? We certainly don't want to be those permissive parents who say, 'I know Johnny hit your son on the head with a rock, but he *needs* to be physically active right now.' (I know such people!) It all starts when a child makes his first 'mistake'. One of Sir Ken Robinson's most appealing quotes is: 'If you're not prepared to be wrong you'll never come up with anything original.'[37] And if we're not prepared to let our children make mistakes, they will never gain the wisdom, the know-how, the social skills and the creativity that comes when we have to fix something that's wrong or broken.

I can't cover every possible parenting situation and how to respond, but there are a few key elements that might become useful tools for raising children who are resilient, compassionate, intelligent beings who will not have an over-active stress response to the world. In Australia, on a live television show called *Insight*, the topic of smacking children was up for discussion. I was surprised at how many parents believed that spanking children was the only way to teach our youngest offspring how to behave. I beg to differ. If a pre-verbal toddler is about to touch something hot, we can demonstrate, from the moment we hold our child and turn on the stove, that the glowing red bit is 'OW! Very hot!' Dramatic sounds help but they don't have to be overly loud. If our toddler is actually reaching out to grab something hot, we have to demonstrate again, it's *hot*, and yes, remove him from danger. Though he can't speak, he will only need to see that a few times to get what we mean. We keep the focus on what is essential (the safety of our child) and *not* on his behaviour and whether or not he obeys. Staying away from danger is paramount, but at this point it's not a behaviour issue unless we make it one.

If the situation isn't dangerous, for example, a tug-of-war over a toy with another toddler, neither of these little people has any capacity to understand who got the toy first and how egalitarian values need to be encouraged. We need to quickly find another toy of equal fabulousness and distract *either one* of the tots with it.

If our little ones want to feed themselves, we need to allow them a bit of a struggle, a bit of hit and miss and a lot of mess so they can learn how to master this new skill. And then how we respond to the mess is really important too.

I'm fascinated by the origins of kindness. I believe more and more that how we respond to our youngest children creates the blueprint for their behaviour towards others for the rest of their lives. Children from birth to seven live in a world that is imitative. They copy everything, even our facial expressions.

When my eleven-month-old baby first pinched my nose, most likely just because it stuck out and was interesting, I showed him immediately I was sore and sad and needed comfort. I could have yelled, 'No! Naughty!' and right there, I could pretty much have guaranteed that he would do it again to see if I reacted with the same anger. He tried it one more time, but I saw it coming and made a sad face before he got the chance. He immediately put his head on my shoulder, 'comforted me', and never did it again.

So, the first and most important tool is *empathy*. If we model it, they'll get it. Even very tiny children understand this. If we *show* them something is hot, they will react as we do. They read our emotions and remember them. If we show them something is hurtful and demonstrate how to give comfort, they will learn empathy. If they spill something/ break something/take something that they shouldn't, we should never over-react. We need to model what we want to see. If a cup of juice is spilled, we might get two cloths, one for ourselves and one for our toddler. If a sibling or friend has been hurt, we might take our child by the hand to help make the hurt person better. If we yell angrily, 'Now go and apologise!' at our preschooler, he will learn our *anger* relating to the friend he's just hurt, while what we really want is that he feels *empathy* for the hurt friend. If a four-year-old has dropped a puppy into the toilet bowl to see if it will swim, we might swallow our distress, remove the puppy and explain that baby animals don't like this at all. We should make sure the four-year-old warms and dries the puppy in a towel on her lap and makes it better again.

If we do this when our children are young, they will develop into well-adjusted people. The most important thing we need to remember is that we have to be *consistent*. If we're empathetic one minute and yelling with fury the next, our children will become confused and mistrustful.

Most of us are guilty of being overly intellectual in response to our youngest children at one time or another, but it causes a great deal of stress for some. It seems innocuous, and we often think we're doing our kids a favour, but I've seen enough preschoolers who suffer the results of over-intellectualising adults burdening them with information that is inappropriate.

Three-year-olds to six-year-olds constantly ask 'why'. Why is Dad at work? Why is the sky blue? Why is the sun yellow? Remember, their brains are developing, growing and very, very far from complete. This is a phase of enormous physical growth. Everything is happening: bones and brains and muscles are all learning to do the things that will enable the body to be a functionally excellent specimen. It's a heavy burden for a young child to be told that the sun is yellow because it's really a ball of burning gas under constant nuclear fusion and that the light's particular frequency combined with earth's atmosphere results in yellow … yet we give our children those explanations often on a daily basis without considering that the brain is not equipped to process abstractions at this point. A preschooler's emotional life needs careful and appropriate nurturing. We don't need to mould our youngest children into mini-academics. It stresses and taxes their capacities.

An answer for a child under seven needs to speak to her imagination. The answer to the sun question could be that the sun is yellow because it's warm, and when we are in the sunshine it makes us warm. Creative, imaginative, image-rich responses will feed their growing brains. We shouldn't lie, but we have to give them the right response at the right time that will satisfy them. We do our youngest children a big favour when we keep things simple and creative, and when we make a point of remembering how beautiful and good the world appears to be to those who are still so new in it.

Likewise, children this age hear and absorb adult conversation, which can sometimes be an enormous stressor. Last weekend, a three-year-old said to his mother at a restaurant table next to ours, 'Daddy's not here because Daddy has girlfriends and so he doesn't live with us anymore.' That's a pretty heavy and stressful burden for a three-year-old who has no idea about adult transgressions, divorce or separation. Children younger than seven equally don't need to know about terrorist attacks and why America's foreign policy in the Middle East is decidedly unpopular there. Conversations about sex, drugs and rock 'n' roll can wait until quite a bit later. And yet so often we don't guard our children's innocence (or take note of the conversations they overhear) and we catapult them early into the adult world. It's worth repeating again that the earlier children develop an over-active stress response to the world, the earlier that gets written into neural circuitry and the harder it is to undo.

In young children, the corpus callosum, which joins the two hemispheres of the brain, is still maturing. Neural networks are slowly developing. Expecting young children to be reasonable, logical and consequential during this phase can easily create stress. They are not cause-and-effect beings. Their 'species' experiences the wonder of a world bright with colour, alive with beautiful possibility and full of magical things. Expecting children of this age to perceive things magically and imaginatively is probably right on the money.

Remember that this age group copies everything, especially what we do as parents. Remember, too, that these developing little bodies need to move: *play* is this age group's work. It's what they need. Most importantly, if we parents stay consistent, loving and empathetic in these early years, the rewards later on will be exponential.

Seven to fourteen

Between seven and fourteen, children are insatiably curious about the world and about people. It's so important during this phase for us to keep our cool. The seven- to fourteen-year-old is no longer in that imitative phase. If our nine-year-olds watch us sweeping the floor and washing the dishes, they (sadly) won't simply imitate. We have to ask (politely) for some assistance.

My mantra is 'Maintain Sainthood' or at least give it a good shot, even when emotional tsunamis threaten our equilibrium! Our children will push boundaries but it's never too late to respond with empathy and honesty. Again, consistency is the key. If we fly off the handle and become The Great Dictator in response to one situation, and then go soft as melted cheese and give in, in another, our kids will play us for all we're worth. It really helps to have a partner or spouse on the same page. It seems essential to me that we actively discuss parenting styles and decide with our partners what *outcome* we want in any given situation.

These outcomes need to be positive, as in, *I really want Amy and Michael to play together nicely*, and NOT, *I really want to punish Amy for hurting Michael so she can see the consequences of her bad behaviour.* The first desired outcome will have us behaving with empathy and honesty, and the likely result is that we'll have socially well-adjusted and sympathetic people in our family. The second outcome will have us behaving like dictators and will encourage our children to become rebels and in-fighters. The first approach results in a low-stress environment. The second approach — you guessed it — causes Stress Central.

If partners have different parenting styles, this can be very stressful for children. Consistency is the key, remember. Empathy with *each other* is the first step on the way to creating a low-stress home environment. And of course, parents arguing with each other about decisions *relating to* children *in front of* children — *You shouldn't have let him watch TV,*

I'd already told him he couldn't! — will guarantee dissonance and quickly teach our children that they can play us off against one another.

I would make a huge effort to keep criticisms out of earshot of the kids … and then count to ten before actually voicing them. Perhaps it's *not* always necessary to chew out a partner or interfere in how our other half handles situations. A child's connection to each parent is unique and valid, and if the objective is to create a low-stress emotional environment for our children, I'd aim for the broader discussion of what our values are as parents and what we want for our kids, and then back right off and allow each other to parent, trusting that we share the same love, the same desires for how we want our children to grow up.

If arguments of any kind do arise in front of the children, research has established that if children witness the *resolution* of those arguments, and the re-establishment of harmony in the home, then the negative effects are mitigated to a large degree.[38] Still, arguing *about* how we parent our children *in front* of them is a guaranteed stressor on our children, and we have the intellectual capacity as adults to choose not to do that.

In this middle part of childhood, the size of the frontal lobes in the brain increases, the corpus callosum goes through more maturation, and neural networks between brain hemispheres develop, enabling children to think in an increasingly systematic, integrated way. So, at this point in time, if we want to discuss in a little more detail why the sun is yellow, we can. By fourteen our children could easily engage in an exciting discussion about the difference between nuclear fission and fusion, but I'd still be *more* imaginative and *less* scientific with my eight-year-old on the sun question. Remember, we are still supporting our children's slow movement out into the world and the gradual maturation of their nervous systems. The more our responses take into account their physiological, emotional and cognitive development, the less stress we place on our growing children.

Fifteen to adult

This age group is possibly the one about which parents feel the most trepidation. Teens are the most maligned and the least understood. Fifteen- to eighteen-year-olds can appear terrifying. They are large and strong and sometimes loud and obnoxious; they often swear; they take risks that turn parents' hearts cold, and on the streets, people give them a wide berth and try not to catch their eyes.

And yet, these almost-adults are at most risk out of all groups of youngsters for self-harm and suicide.

How we parent our teens is as important as how we parented our newborns. My friend Mary has two daughters, Joanna, thirteen and Anna, fifteen, and had a high-powered job in the real-estate business. She worked six days a week, sometimes fifteen hours a day, and she seemed to have boundless energy. But recently Joanna developed a lump on her collarbone, and before it was diagnosed as a bone infection, Mary was told to prepare for the worst. (I wonder how on earth that advice was supposed to help her. It seems absolutely counter-intuitive and catapulted her into a nightmare world.) The experience threw her life into sharp focus. As a dedicated mother and hard-worker, she had had her eyes fixed on the goal: make enough money, buy the dream house with a bit of land, which would enable them to finally get the puppy that Joanna has been begging for, and so on. 'I just realised,' she said, 'that I've lost sight of what's really important. Sure the house and the puppy would be nice, but me spending time with my girls would be much nicer. Everything has to change. Although I thought my kids would need me less as they hit their teens, I realise they need me more. They have big things to work through. I'm also aware that when I call them from work I'm always barking at them, *Have you eaten? Have you done your homework?* — all that kind of thing. Our relationship is reduced to being about all these functions and I realised I've lost sight of what it's all about. I've just quit my job. I might get something else that gives me proper weekends and allows me to work normal hours, but I'm focusing on the girls and doing things together. In a few short years they'll be moving out into the world and I really want to enjoy them and be there with them.'

Contrary to the swaggering bravado and attitude that so many teens seem to exhibit, they are, for the most part, in desperate need of affirmation, love and acceptance. I love these half-adults and remember vividly what it was like to be there. I give the adolescents in my life a lot of my time; I am genuinely interested in them and love to spend time with them. I don't patronise them and I'm not trying to be their friend. I'm aware that my interest means a lot to them. I've seen many students go from being de-motivated and depressed to feeling inspired and capable, simply as a result of an adult showing interest and belief in who they are and what they're doing. Teens need to know that adults believe in them. It's crucial for their emotional health. We also have to know how to begin to let them go.

'I don't want my mum to be my buddy,' said one of my fifteen-year-old students. 'I want her to keep her authority. But not as a sergeant major. She overprotects me and doesn't know how to move on with me. I'm not five anymore and she doesn't know what to do with that.'

It's in their teens that our children will begin to show signs of wear and tear if they've been stressed for a long time. It's also in their teens that our children begin to show us the results of our parenting and their response to that parenting and their environments during the preceding years … for better or worse.

David Garb, a well-known New Zealand therapist, explained in a recent lecture in Australia on the teen–parent relationship that, in order to maintain healthy and low-stress relationships with our teens, we need to be absolutely clear and explicit about *our own* needs, and never assume that 'teens should *know*'. If we need our sixteen-year-old to take out the rubbish, the conversation could be: 'I'm pretty exhausted, James. Would you be able to take out the rubbish?' This is preferable to, 'Please take out the rubbish now', which is not a *request* but a *command*, and which, despite the fact that we've inserted a 'please', leaves our teens feeling as though there really isn't an option to say, 'Not now', or 'Sure, later'. As adults, we have the right to refuse to do something, yet we often command our teens as though they have no right of refusal — and this lends itself to classic teen rebellion.[39]

What we want is a teen who will do things not because he *has* to but because he *chooses* to, because he understands that he is *giving* something (in this case, help) and that it is genuinely appreciated. Empathy is the quality we rely on here, and if we haven't built it from the outset, though it's not too late to begin, it's going to take time, patience and absolute consistency to develop.

This is the age group that begins to suffer from what I set out to describe at the beginning of this book. It's an acute stressor that I'd like to term 'Finish Line Syndrome'. When our children are between fourteen and eighteen, we start feeding them *our* anxiety relating to them going out into the world. I understand that, for most of us, it comes from a place of love and concern for their wellbeing. But our children often grow up desperately fearing the Finish Line, which doesn't even exist. After all, we go on learning things for the rest of our lives, and the time we spend at school should be a brief journey, not a high-stakes, high-powered race. We have to do our best to embody values that acknowledge where the world is truly at, and be mindful that we don't inadvertently, or very deliberately, put on the pressure and make our teens feel like they're not good enough, they won't make it and the rest of their lives could be doomed.

In New Zealand, a mother and her seventeen-year-old son were at loggerheads over the son's apparent lack of interest in his $20,000-a-year private school. He was going out on weekends and generally having a good time. His grades were fine but his mother was deeply concerned by the amount of time he spent not doing what he was 'supposed' to be doing. The son just wanted his mother off his case. She was terrified he'd fail and that all that money would be wasted. Eventually the two came to an agreement: the son promised that if he failed he'd pay back all the school fees for that year. The mother promised to stop bothering him about his school work. He continued to party for the rest of the year. She stopped nagging him. He passed with flying colours and the benefit of their decision was far-reaching: their relationship was respectful and intact.

David Garb maintains it's not a bad idea to say (not too lightly, but not too seriously) to your teen, 'So, Jen, how am I doing as a parent?' And then to say, 'And I'll let you know how you're doing as a daughter.'[40] Being able to discuss the ways we relate to each other can really inspire a deepening of trust, understanding and empathy, which are the relationship pillars that can protect our offspring against the effects of long-term stress.

As a parent, I'm guilty of the entire menu of mistakes available in the great restaurant of parenting. But I often apologise and ask for forgiveness and feedback, such as, 'If we get into such a situation again, what can *I* do so that it doesn't spiral into an upset for us both? What can *you* do?' We might agree as a first step not to talk about sensitive issues when we're dog-tired at the end of the day!

Our fifteen- to eighteen-year-olds are often easily our intellectual equals or superiors, at least in *some* areas. But there is a fundamental difference between a fifteen-year-old's brain and an adult's: they lack the wisdom that comes from living in the world and dealing with it for decades. This age group can be prone to making absolutely (to us) absurd decisions, engaging in risky behaviour, and often being very sorry for it afterwards. As a teacher I've had the not-so-delightful experience of being party to many situations, and the after-effects of those, that teens get themselves into.

On an international school trip, one of my students got upset with someone else in the class at eleven o'clock at night and went out for 'a breath of fresh air'. Half an hour later she had disappeared into a foreign city. It was freezing cold, she was in her socks and a flimsy shirt, and I was imagining the worst, knowing that in this city, just two weeks before, two young women had been assaulted. I would never, in a million years, have wandered off alone like she did. A week later, in a serious meeting, she expressed what I knew to be true: she literally 'had no idea' what she was doing until she started walking back to the backpackers' lodge, and she was very contrite about how that had affected those who were supposed to be responsible for her during the trip. Consequences were a week's suspension and an agreement signed by all that would enable the student, over the next months, to keep to certain behaviours and re-establish the trust that she'd broken, giving her an opportunity to think more carefully about every decision.

In a discussion on how stress is, in fact, worse for teen brains than for adult brains, study researcher Adriana Galvan at the University of California in Los Angeles spoke to *ScienceNatio*, an online publication run by the National Science Foundation (NSF), and said, 'Teenagers experience stress as more stressful [than adults] … Their risk-taking is due to the immaturity of the prefrontal cortex, which is responsible for *regulating* behaviour and *anticipating* consequences.'[41]

The link between stress and risky behaviour has a neurological underpinning. 'The teenagers show more activation in the reward system than adults when making risky choices,' Galvan states. So, if a teen is experiencing an emotionally loaded moment, the ability to assess risk is severely diminished. 'When you are stressed out as a teenager, it's interfering with your ability to make decisions. It's interfering with how the brain functions in regions that are still developing, mainly the reward system and the prefrontal cortex.' Stress inhibits the teen brain's ability to process and foresee consequences.[42]

Our young adults still need us to be the dependable, loving, empathetic individuals we were when they were infants. In this way, we can minimise the risks they face as teens. We are still an intricate, essential and responsible factor in the construction of their psychological environment.

KEY POINTS

- As parents we make up a significant portion of our children's psychological/emotional environment.

- Over-intellectualising stresses children between zero and seven. The brain is not mature enough to cope.

- Arguing about parenting decisions in front of children is an acute stressor.

- Being explicit about what we need from our teens is beneficial.

- Stress is more stressful for teens because of how the prefrontal cortex is maturing: stress interferes with the ability to anticipate consequences.

FINDING THE RIGHT EDUCATIONAL ENVIRONMENT

As new concepts such as 'emotional intelligence' become more widely applied and understood, more educators are realising that cognitive ability is not the sole or necessarily the most critical determinant of young people's aptitude to flourish in today's society.[43] As the educational landscape changes, this will have to become more the norm and less the exception. So, though we're still mostly locked into an archaic educational model that is geared towards one-sided academic development, there is a lot we can do both at home and with our children's teachers that can minimise stress and support our children's psychological, physical and neurological development as they make their way in the world.

In this chapter I will investigate ways in which we can select the kind of educational environment that won't unduly stress our children. Sometimes we find the right environment and that does it all. Sometimes it's about making compromises and arrangements with the people in an environment so that our children are protected to the best of our ability.

Preschool

For our smallest children, once it's time to send them to preschool and kindergarten, we need to understand all the basics of their physical development and find a school that supports that. I personally would not send my child to an accelerated learning program where the focus is on academics. I've visited prestigious little schools in England where the focus for four-year-olds is highly academic. Art appreciation and identifying how you *feel* in response to a story is meaningless and pretty joyless to a four-year-old. I would search for the kindergarten or preschool that makes creative play a focused priority. The school needs to offer an outside play area and lots of time to be in it.

I would look for a school that does not tax my child's slowly developing brain before it is ready. The emotions our young children feel need to be positive. Joy, anticipation, wonder, excitement are all part of the picture. Remember, we're talking about children whose brains are not fully myelinated. Any early academic skills that they have are splinter skills, not an indication of real global intellectual capacity.

It is essential to protect our small children from as many stressors as possible *for as long as we can.* The question we should ask is not *whether* they will meet some of the harsher realities of this world (they will), but *how* and *when* they do.

As parents of young children we're given this gift of a few years in which we're actually able to select the place we think will be optimum to our child's development. And the people who work in that environment are key. Are they warm and loving? When we meet them, do we get a good 'vibe'? We need to know we are leaving our children in a lovingly coherent place, because a child who is surrounded by a low-stress nurturing environment will not over-react to stressful situations later.

For young children, I would seek out an environment that supports their physical development, that does not focus on introducing early academics, and where I can literally 'feel the love'. This will support their growth in an optimal way.

Primary school

When our children go on to primary school, we should keep in mind that their surroundings should still support them developmentally. Sometimes, this is really tricky: classrooms are often designed as though they're *promoting* the ADHD factors in students and teachers alike, as I experienced in Florida.

We need to meet the teachers who will be spending most of the day with our children, and we need to feel good about them and as if we can have a supportive relationship with that person. If we feel anxious about or antagonistic towards a child's teacher, I guarantee that our children will detect that anxiety and its source. If we simply can't feel good about the teacher, we should seriously consider another school.

It's also really helpful for us to let go of prejudices and preconceived notions about educational institutions, and assess each one that we look at with sensitivity: is *this place* and *this teacher* a good fit for my child? Each child is unique, so word-of-mouth generalisations might need serious re-evaluation when it comes to considering a school's suitability for a particular child. I've had to let go of all my preconceptions about different forms of education. I am deeply grateful that there are many options available, because there is no 'one size fits all' school system.

So, if we believe passionately and hard-headedly that we need to support public education, no matter what, we might have a torturous journey at some point when we discover that the best fit for a child is a small, private school. Likewise, if we look down from a dizzy height on public schools and decide that our children will only attend the best, most highly regarded private schools, we could well be setting ourselves up for a very stressful journey if the values and aims of that system don't end up suiting our sons or daughters.

When we first moved to Australia, we put our son in three different primary schools in the first year. It was quite traumatic. I looked at his behaviour, his daily headaches, his reluctance to go to school every day, and then I looked closely at his physical and emotional environments. He was fine on the weekends but falling apart during the week. The difference lay in the *environment* and the *people* he experienced in each of those environments. As we switched from school to school, I gently told him to see each experience as an experiment. I said, 'Remember, there's nothing trapping you here. Give it a go, and if it doesn't work for you, we'll find another option. There are tons of schools and one of them will be the right fit.' Then we found the right fit and it wasn't where I expected it to be. Suffice it to say that I swallowed all my previous prejudices regarding one particular educational system over another (yes, we all harbour those) and embraced the new environment as the right place for my son to thrive.

My friend Nicole, who lives in Florida, has her daughters enrolled in a large 'magnet' public school, which apparently focuses on the arts. In her dealings with other parents she reflects that, 'Most parents feel like it's their duty to push their children as hard as they can *all* of the time. I'm the only parent whose child qualified for gifted services who declined it … because, I said, I don't want my child stressed, and I want to know whether it will stress her. The teachers had never *ever* encountered anyone who *refused* gifted services! There's so much focus on grades here that a ten-year-old in my daughter's class who got a 'B' in her report said her mom 'about killed her'. I've assured my daughters that I'm proud of the people they are and that grades are insignificant.'

I asked her about the structure of the school day, and she said, 'What they do is they avoid recess [break time]. Recess is rare. If it does occur it lasts only two to four minutes. There's a concerted effort to avoid any social interaction between children. It keeps bullying and other issues at bay. Children are over-stimulated in the classroom the whole day. They're not given any time to socially connect or interact. No talking is allowed. They can whisper and chat in small groups about work only. If students are walking in the halls, they have to walk in silence, in a row. In the cafeteria, where they have ten minutes to eat, all the children sit and face forward. They can whisper, but anything above a whisper and the lights get flicked and enforced silence follows. After they've eaten, the children go into a dark room where a movie is playing where they wait for their teachers to collect them. The other day my youngest daughter's class was making a noise, so when the teacher came to pick them up from the movie room, the noise report was given to her and she marched the children back to their classroom, taking them past the playground, where she said *you would have had recess, but because you were noisy, you have to go straight back to the classroom.*

Nicole says her children are so wired when they get home that she makes sure their bikes are ready outside the garage. They go for an hour's bike ride. Otherwise, she says, the evening is 'a meltdown'. This is a creative way of mitigating the stress of the day and making sure the children move their bodies and spend time with their parents.

When I asked her why she has her children there, she said, 'This is *good* compared to mainstream America.' (This is someone who has, more thoroughly than anyone else I know, researched schools in her 60-kilometre radius for the past several years and found the best possible place for her children.)

'A few of the teachers are open to some degree. I can talk to them. But I'm thinking of homeschooling my youngest. She's not thriving in this environment. Third grade is the year she's in and it's the year the kids do the FCATs. It's the one grade where they hold you back a year if you fail. The teacher keeps threatening the kids with the words, *you're gonna be held back!* As my youngest starts to understand grades, she's getting upset about what a 'C' means. She's started saying she's fat! She also has no opportunity to forge friendships and no free time. My eldest is coping much better and has a sense of irony about everything. She's also outperforming almost every other student in the school and, for the moment, is fine.'

I asked her why she'd refused the gifted services for her daughter.

'Well, I've said I need to explore it further. I want to know whether *gifted services* mean extra stress. If kids are pulled out of their regular classes, do they have to catch up on what they miss in addition to what they get in the gifted program? Is it really enrichment? My feeling is that it's just pushing them harder. So, I'm going to sit in on the gifted classes and see for myself.'

Here is a parent who might take one child out of a school that seems to be fine for the other child. In addition to that, she's communicating with the teachers so that she knows exactly what's happening with and to her children.

I asked Nicole what she did to support her children in a less than ideal primary-school environment and what she did to assess whether the environment was indeed the right fit for a particular child. Here's what she's done.

'I volunteer in the classroom (that way I see how the teacher interacts with the children and what the day looks like); I interviewed and spoke to the teachers who would be teaching my child; I let teachers know what I wanted. For example, I've said to my daughters' teachers, "Look, we understand that homework is a reality here, however, from my perspective, if there's an opportunity to give less rather than more, please do. I prefer no stress." Maybe they think I'm crazy, but in my mind, it's worth it. I had to advocate for my child and what my family's philosophy is ... if you run into a brick wall, change schools! Be involved. Parents who volunteer get a better sense of the environment and the people in it.'

Children in primary school need to be engaged in activities that support neural development. In the past, children used to do things like knit or play the recorder. These are elements that existed in mainstream education but have been mostly pushed out in favour of iPads and laptops for every child. In doing so we've lost a fundamental developmental step that we might be paying for in other areas.

Activities that engage and support fine-motor skills in primary-school children involve the brain in complex activity that paves the way for the development of neural connections that will be required for later academic skills.

In Finland's educational model, where formal learning begins later than it does in the UK, the US, Australia and many other countries, we might be concerned that this would be occurring relatively late. However, there is absolutely *no proven benefit* at all for children learning to read at age four or five as opposed to seven. Looking at the success of the Finnish system, I'd strongly advocate that educational authorities look to that country for a successful educational model where children are evidently not being hurried towards an imaginary high-stakes finish line, and where the results are inarguably impressive.

Love, patience and understanding for the developmental process itself will alleviate parental stress in the early grades. So, look for a school that understands that children develop at different rates and that works with differentiated learning approaches. This means that the school is aware that there are visual learners, kinaesthetic learners and auditory learners, and offers learning opportunities that suit all those preferred styles of learning across the board. It means a school where brain maturation is understood as a slow process that will take up to 25 years to complete. Find a primary school where children are valued and where it's obvious that there is a variety of activities to support the development of gross- and fine-motor skills, that engage the children in creative activities that bring joy and harmony to their lives (music, art, drama, dance) as well the normal academic program. Experiential learning, as we all know, is one of the most significant ways in which we develop the capacity to do something well.

Remember that heart rhythms are affected by activities that regulate breathing: rowing a boat, dancing, singing, playing a wind instrument, reciting poetry or Shakespeare all affect the breathing and, thus, the heart. Primary schools that offer these activities, including Waldorf/ Steiner schools and Montessori, would be absolutely worth considering. We don't have to find Utopia, but we can go a long way to minimising the stressful impact on our children.

Outside of school, engage *with* children physically and creatively as much as possible, expanding on all these elements. Kayaking together as a family on the weekend, playing games like cards or tag, making a family member a birthday card or building a go-kart all create strong warm relationships and allow children the space they need to develop into well-balanced human beings.

High school

When we come to look for the ideal high-school environment for our teens, we need to consider that they find what *they* are looking for, what inspires *them*, as well as what *we* believe they need. For that to happen, we might take a step back and engage our teens in a conversation that takes into account the following:

- Does the environment look like somewhere where you can be happy spending your day? (Is it aesthetically appealing?)
- Do the teachers seem genuine?
- Do you feel like you will count?

- **Does the curriculum offer things that interest/inspire you?**

In fact, the research we need to do for high school is the same as for primary school, but our teens need to be much more engaged in the decision-making process. We need to support them to find an environment where they are not treated like inmates in an institution. An excellent but highly academic school might be just the thing for one teen but inordinately stressful for another. Choosing an environment that is supportive of our teen's development needs to match who they are as a person. Some young people need a school with 2000 others, while others thrive in smaller schools. It's essential that during this period, when almost anything outside of serious academic work is regarded as superfluous, we adults ensure our teens are getting the space and time to breathe out, to follow their creative impulses, to daydream, to do physical activity, to play music and spend time with friends. If we can balance these elements, we will be supporting their development in an optimum way, in optimum environments, and mitigating the effects of the stresses they will face.

For the turbulent teens, finding a school that is aesthetically pleasing and tells them they are welcome and trusted, a place where they are treated with respect, where activities are offered that inspire them and challenge them, rather than terrify and oppress them, is ideal. And this place could be anywhere.

The people in this place will be affecting our teens, so their values, their state of heart will impact how our children feel. As we know, the IHM has measured the role of 'physiological coherence in the detection and measurement of cardiac energy exchange between people. When an individual is generating a coherent heart rhythm, synchronization between that individual's brainwaves and another person's heartbeat is more likely to occur.'[44] This is still absolutely true for our teens. We know without a doubt that the physiological factors that ensure proper cognitive, emotional and intellectual development are intimately linked with the heart and with the healthy function of the autonomic nervous system. Clarity of thought is not just randomly associated with feeling good. Brain function is optimised when the rhythmic systems in the body are operating in coherence with one another. A person in high coherence is not a stressed person.

It's during the teen years that the phrase 'use it or lose it' is particularly apt. The brain is going through a rapid pruning phase and those neural connections that aren't used are pruned. If our teens are sitting glued to the screen lost in some addictive computer game, then it doesn't take a high-powered scientist to figure out that those thumb–eye connections will be in excellent working order, while the ability to speak a foreign language or play an instrument might be relegated to the back seat or vanish altogether. So, I would support teens to move through the world and engage as much and as often as possible with new things *that they love*. This in itself is a stress protector and will ensure their brains continue to develop optimally.

KEY POINTS

- A child surrounded by a nurturing, low-stress environment will not over-react to stressful situations later.

- Look for an early-childhood environment that focuses on physical development and creative play rather than early academics.

- Look for a primary school that offers differentiated learning approaches and understands the needs of this age group's physical development; one that also welcomes volunteers and parent involvement.

- Look for a high school that inspires and challenges teens and makes them feel like they matter.

- Seek out environments where the people are warm and positive. The state of their hearts will affect our children.

STOPPING STRESS
IN ITS TRACKS

Teaching our children to manage their own reactions to situations will give them life-long tools. Children from the age of eight or nine can learn to completely stop themselves in the midst of a stressful moment. It requires a degree of mindfulness, but it's something that youngsters should know how to do. (And so should we!) Here are the steps:[45]

1. Focus on your breathing and count to about six as you breathe in and seven as you breathe out.

2. As you begin to breathe evenly (without trying too hard), bring your attention to the area of the heart. Fill each in-breath with the thought or picture of something that you love, something that makes you feel deep gratitude. It could be a person, a lovely day or something affirming that someone said.

3. Sustain this for five minutes.

If our children can learn to sustain this for just a few minutes, the fight-or-flight effect will be over. They will have actually stopped the sympathetic nervous system from running away with itself and will have activated the parasympathetic nervous system instead. I've used this trick before stressful meetings, in the midst of noisy and chaotic class-rooms and at home. It's much easier than one might think to maintain saint-like calm even when the situation around us might look ominously like the precursor to the end of the world!

The EmWave is biofeedback technology created by the research-ers and neurocardiologists at the IHM. It allows users to *watch* their ECGs (electrocardiograms) on a home computer and monitor them-selves going from low coherence to high coherence. I use this technol-ogy in my classroom, at home and in presentations across the country to demonstrate the powerful effects we can have on our heart rhythms and stress levels.

I've also used the EmWave to experiment with which activities sup-port high coherence. One experiment involved the manual arts/wood-work teacher at a school in Cincinnati, Ohio. I was running a workshop on stress and children, and he told me that when children were 'acting up' in class they were sent to him. He would then set up the shave horse, which is a kind of rowing machine: you put a piece of wood in the front and as you 'row', you shave off big slices of wood that peel off like but-ter. Children who were sent to him were allowed to work on the shave horse for fifteen to twenty minutes. The teacher said that the rhythmical action, which was quite physically demanding, as well as the repetitive aspect of the activity and the satisfaction you get from shaving off big slices of wood that then curl onto the floor cleared up behaviour issues. Fifteen minutes on that, he said, and the kids were calm and centred, ready to go back to class.

Behaviour issues correlate directly with over-active sympathetic nervous system activity, so what seemed to be happening on the shave horse was that, through the rhythmical activity, the children's breath-ing was affected and regulated. This then had a regulating effect on the heart, the brain and all other systems. In effect, the activity on the shave horse enabled the children to 'recalibrate' their nervous systems.

When I mentioned the concept of 'high coherence' to this teacher, he was convinced that after a few minutes of being on the shave horse, he would be in precisely this state. We put him to the test. He worked away for five minutes and then I hooked him up to sensors and we watched his heart rhythms on the screen. They were immediately ordered and coherent. He was, indeed, in a state of high coherence. I tried it myself and the result was the same. A few minutes on the shave horse had me sweating but enjoying the experience and afterwards my heart rhythms too were ordered and coherent.

It's a radical suggestion, but I honestly wonder whether we shouldn't replace detention rooms in schools across the world with rooms full of shave horses, and get rid of the 'naughty corner' at home and replace it with a shave horse in the garage. Behaviour management does not address the physiological issues children might be experiencing when they 'act up', not one little bit. But the shave horse does.

The IHM tools, overall, have already positively changed the lives of thousands of stressed-out youngsters. The IHM undertook a major research study when they introduced a program called TestEdge in schools across the US, supported by the Department of Education. Based on self-regulation and heart-focused breathing, and using the EmWave, the study looked at the results of 980 high-school students who were given the opportunity to use the biofeedback tools to manage stress and test-related anxiety. The students significantly reduced their test-related anxiety and there was parallel improvement in their standardised test results. 'Overall, the evidence from this rich combination of physiological, quantitative and qualitative data indicates that among other successes TestEdge produced substantial physiological, psychological, academic and social benefits for the participants.'[46]

Understanding that we can stop a stressful reaction in its tracks using simple breathing and a loving, grateful thought is as important for our children as it is for us. So what are some other ways that we can help our children to regulate their breathing in such a way that there is a positive impact on the whole nervous system?

In order for anyone to get into a state of high coherence, an activity that regulates breathing is important, because this will enable a corresponding emotional shift. Joy, appreciation and gratitude are powerful catalysts for changing a stressful heart rhythm pattern into one that is highly coherent.

Rhythmical exercise

Rhythmical physical activity changes and regulates breathing and heart rate. Following on from the shave horse, there are other activities that have a very similar effect. We know exercise reduces stress, but some forms of exercise are more conducive to affecting the breathing in a regulatory way. Rowing, Tai Chi, yoga and various other forms of movement affect breathing in a positive way. The focus in these activities is on the breath, or such measured rhythmical movement that a measured breathing pattern results. Add joy or gratitude to the experience and we have the basis for proper stress relief.

Pounding the pavement in a head-rattling jog is good for our physiology when we're stressed, simply because our bodies get to use the glucose and blood flow to the limbs set in motion by the sympathetic nervous system that is kicked into gear when we are stressed. But pavement-pounding does not, of itself, create ordered and regular breathing, nor will many other forms of aerobic exercise. So, telling our kids to take a run when they're feeling overwhelmed is not going to dissolve their anxiety, and while having a good dose of sport in a school program is healthy, it is perhaps not more important than art or music, or ten minutes of heart-focused breathing while actively feeling gratitude, when it comes to impacting the effects of stress.

Music

It's no secret that music changes the brain. Playing any instrument engages many parts of ourselves but when we're young we're unaware of how many things are going on: fingers have to be in the right place; sometimes the breath has to be regulated; the tune has to be right; everyone has to play together. Music, according to world-renowned neuroscientist Oliver Sacks (and author of *Awakenings* and *The Man Who Mistook his Wife for a Hat*, among others) affects more areas of the brain than any other discipline. It is, he says, the only 'discipline' that actually changes the physical appearance of the brain. We are designed for music, for '... its complex sonic patterns woven in time, its logic, its momentum, its unbreakable sequences ...'[47]

In Sarasota, a friend of mine who is a well-respected paediatrician and an accomplished singer was fascinated by the idea of high coherence and the software developed by IHM. She wanted to see what would happen if I recorded her heart rhythms *while* she sang and practised for an upcoming performance of Handel's *Messiah*. She had to sing and stay very still at the same time, a tricky requirement but necessary, since the slightest movement usually resulted in the sensor losing track of the pulse. Fortunately, she was a model volunteer. As she sang, we monitored her coherence ratios. At first she was in low coherence, which is fairly normal for most people most of the time. But then, every time she sang high, extended notes, her heart rhythms became highly coherent. During these stages her out-breath was far longer than her in-breath, but the phrasing was regular and, most importantly, she was in a heightened state of pure enjoyment. The result was clear: singing can create an immediate state of high coherence.

Music/singing and rhythmical activity have an immediate effect on the nervous system because of the way they affect breathing. When positive emotions are added, a state of high coherence can be attained.

So, schools where music is part of the curriculum would offer students a built-in opportunity to spend time in a physiological state that is coherent and not stressed. Alternatively, participating in any kind of music outside of school is just as good. Obviously, if our children are stressed by music lessons or participation, then the benefits are cancelled — and we have to look at what we're doing that makes such a thing stressful; we have to create a situation where the instrument and the music brings enough joy into our children's lives that they want to participate.

My son attends a public school in Australia with 1500 other individuals. The school has a Music Excellence program, which means that the students enrolled in it spend many hours during the week playing, rehearsing and having music lessons. At the high school's recent end-of-year awards night, about 80 per cent of the students who received awards for academic excellence in all subjects were also music students. Those students, who spend more than ten hours of school per week playing all kinds of music, are also almost exclusively untroubled by behaviour issues or distressing social and emotional issues. And their backgrounds are both economically and socially diverse: students come from poor and rich families alike, from homes with same-sex parents, single parent homes and homes where both parents are still together.

Music seems to offer a real opportunity for stress release, for emotional balance and for enhanced academic performance. And yet, generally, when schools have to make budget cuts, all too often music is the first extraneous item to be deleted from the picture. It's as if it's a nice but entirely non-essential curriculum area. We should perhaps take more notice of recent research in Australia by Professor Brian Caldwell for The Song Room, a national non-profit organisation that provides free music and arts-based programs for children in disadvantaged and high-need communities, highlighting discoveries that if anything should inspire calls for the mandatory inclusion of arts and music-based activities in all classrooms (not just music specialty programs).[48]

In a dinosaur move that counters everything we know about the dubious value of high-stakes testing, Australia decided a few years ago to administer national tests every year to every student in years 3, 5, 7 and 9. The tests, known as NAPLAN (National Assessment Program — Literacy And Numeracy), cause a serious amount of stress across the continent. Using comparative data from schools that participated in The Song Room programs and schools that did not, then School Education Minister Peter Garrett commented that, despite the stresses of the exam, the participating schools:

> '... show a higher score for reading, writing,
> spelling, grammar and punctuation, and numeracy.
> The research also shows that schools participating
> in The Song Room programs had better school
> attendance rates than non-participating schools,
> with a 65 per cent lower rate of absenteeism for
> students that have participated in The Song Room
> programs.'

Students that participated in The Song Room program longer-term:

- showed significantly higher grades in their academic subjects (English, mathematics, science and technology, and human society) than those that had not participated;
- achieved significantly higher results in reading and overall literacy in the Year 5 NAPLAN tests;

- had significantly higher attendance; and

- were more likely to be at the top two levels of the Social–Emotional Wellbeing Index in respect of the indicators of resilience, positive social skills, positive work management and engagement skills.[49]

Music offers one of the most powerful antidotes to stress, in terms of the physiological and emotional effects of both participating in it and listening to it. If more schools and parents saw music as an essential part of existence, as opposed to a 'boutique' addition or a specialty subject for talented individuals, our youngsters might show very different trends to the ones we're currently experiencing from them.

What I hope we can all keep in mind is that there is so much we can do to stop the unhealthy trajectory towards stress and disease on which we've inadvertently placed the children we love so much.

The solution to the current crisis in education, the disconnect experienced by teens, the falling standards in schools, the rise in young suicide and worldwide heart disease, is neither obscure nor out of reach. Love, nurturing and appreciation (the opposites of stress and fear) are powerful agents of transformation for growing human beings, both at home and in educational settings.

The environment impacts our children every day and plays a critical role in their physiological, emotional and cognitive development. We, the adults who make up the society that is part of the environment surrounding our children as they grow, can either support our children's development or impede it.

A stressful environment has consequences that go far beyond the unpleasantness of the moment for the children in that environment. If the adults of the world brought more awareness of the effects of love, care and appreciation into our dealings with our children, we could go a long way to begin addressing the pressing needs of the younger generation. As a result, a healthier, more compassionate, coherent and intelligent society might have a chance of evolving.

KEY POINTS

- Using a simple breathing regulation technique stops the stress response in its tracks.

- Activities that regulate our breathing, such as rowing or working on a shave horse, can create high coherence.

- Singing can result in high coherence.

- Music changes the brain.

- Research shows that music programs can lead to dramatic academic and social improvement in students.

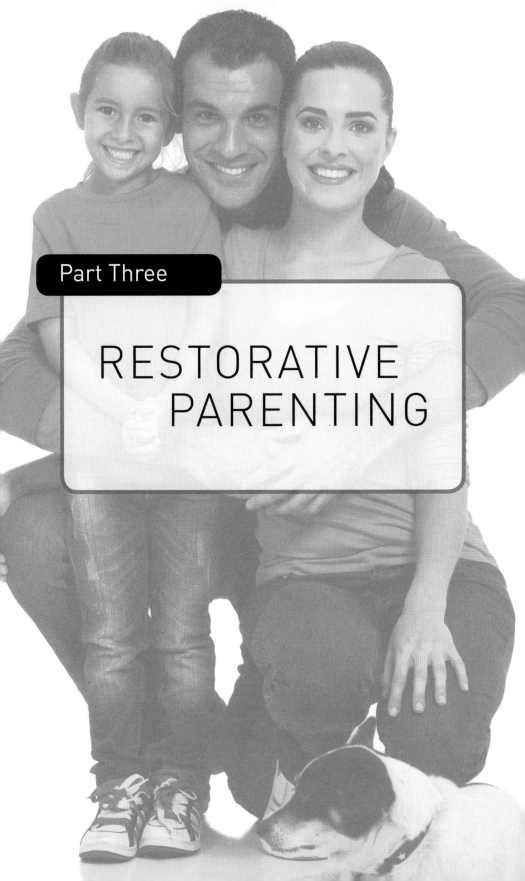

Part Three

RESTORATIVE PARENTING

PARENTING FOR A LOW-STRESS HOME

We parents gain most of our wisdom at the University of Hard Knocks and in the fires of experience. We're wise after we've made our mistakes and have had the benefit of hindsight to acknowledge those disasters. Very little of the true wisdom we call our own is gathered from books or workshops, but in my experience as a parent and a teacher and as a facilitator of Restorative Practice, I've now come across tools that are so empowering that I want every parent to have them. These tools have been around for thousands of years in indigenous cultures, but they have been given new life in contemporary education and parenting models, as a result of innovations in the criminal justice setting.

Such tools are essential if we want to support our children and our families to circumvent the stresses of our modern world. And when we get the fundamentals in place, everything we do becomes more conscious, more restorative, less stressful. We do, however, have to understand a few things before we use these tools: we have to know our own history, acknowledge why we parent the way we do, and understand that the landscape of parenting has historically been more violent and shocking in many respects than we might imagine. For, as parents, we have been committing crimes of one kind or another against our children since the very beginning.

The nature of Restorative Practice is simply this: *to repair any harm that has been done and restore relationships. The focus is on the relationship, not on the 'crime', or on the person who commits the 'crime'.* It was used successfully first in the criminal justice system, enabling victims of crimes to meet the perpetrators and allow them to experience the full human result of the crimes that had been committed. It gave criminals an opportunity to attempt to repair some of the harm, and to engage with the people they had hurt.

In South Africa, after the end of apartheid, the Truth and Reconciliation Commission was a harrowing restorative impulse that allowed thousands of victims of apartheid atrocities to meet the perpetrators of some of the worst human rights abuses. An unprecedented catharsis took place in that country which I haven't seen equalled anywhere in the world, resulting in amnesty, forgiveness and closure. South Africa, long a pariah in the world because of its racist politics, is now probably the most culturally integrated place I have ever seen.

Restorative Practice has now moved into schools and homes, and is being used very effectively around the world. The International Institute for Restorative Practices in Pennsylvania runs high-level training courses for people who work in a variety of settings.

Recently I attended a workshop on restorative parenting run by expert facilitator Margaret Thorsborne, entitled 'Parenting for a Peaceful Home'. Here she explored the paradigm of restorative parenting. It's my belief that this is probably by far the most pragmatic and sensible approach if we want to eliminate the element of stress from our family dynamics.

'There's a burden inherent in being a parent,' Thorsborne states. Most of us who are good, loving parents feel guilty about the parenting trials that burden us, guilty about reaching the end of our tethers, and guilty for sometimes wishing that we could just get a first-class ticket to a tropical island where no children are allowed.

In referencing the work of Australian psycho-historian Robin Grille, Margaret told us that, through the ages, parents have responded in many ways to this burden. Historically, the family has been a place where some of the most appalling crimes have been committed against children. Between the fourth and fourteenth centuries, 20 to 25 per cent of children were victims of infanticide. When people began to grow squeamish about murdering their own children, acts of abandonment increased. Children were dumped, sent away, given to wet nurses, sold into slavery. These unimaginable crimes were committed in primitive attempts to 'relieve the burden of parenting'.[1]

These crimes still exist. Not in the same proportion, but they still happen worldwide, every single day. Infanticide is still a problem in many countries. Abandonment is rife, though there are many degrees and numerous ways of doing it; these days, even children sent away too early to boarding school, or who spend most of their days in day care from an early age, can be suffering the effects of parental abandonment. 'These children often don't get the opportunity to attach emotionally to a loving adult.'[2]

Our instinctive parenting styles are often a response to our own upbringing, to our expectations and fantasies about what makes a 'good' parent or what makes a 'good' child, and so, if we look at the different generations, we might say that each generation of parenting is a reaction to the previous one. If the 1950s produced a generation of parents who were strict and authoritarian, then the sixties and seventies saw reactions to this and children were raised in a permissive style. And so on.

These days, ask any parent what their burdens are and you'll get a response that is really easy to relate to. At the restorative parenting workshop, responses were as follows. It's a burden when:

- my child doesn't listen

- my child is cheeky

- my child is insulting

- my children fight with each other.

When Margaret asked these parents what their responses were to these burdens, one mother of twins said that, if her children were fighting with each other, she'd send them to the laundry to think about what they'd done. The idea of the laundry eventually became traumatic and her kids would howl, 'Nooooooo! Not the laundry!' So, now she separates them and sends each one to a different room. Another parent had a time-out step. A mother of teenagers said she took away privileges like the use of the computer or their mobile phones if the teens misbehaved or broke the rules of the household. All these, of course, are forms of punishment.

Our most primitive and basic response to children's 'bad' behaviour is retributive. No one wants to be insulted, ignored, treated rudely and badly by the people we love most and bring into the world. Nor do we, as parents, want to live in houses where we have no control over the behaviour of our children. Our biggest fear is losing control, not having the authority to raise our children properly or give them the values they need to get on in the world. If they don't listen to us, we cannot keep them safe or live the lives we aspire to live. So, it's accepted almost without question that some form of retributive discipline or punishment will make our children change their behaviour. In this model, we focus on a) what rule was broken b) who's to blame and c) what punishment is deserved.

Parents in the workshop agreed that they punished their children in order to 'break the cycle', 'make them see what they've done', and 'stop them doing it again'. We use punishment because it's quick; it's what we know; it makes us feel powerful; it satisfies a primitive need for justice; and we believe that chaos will reign if we don't punish. Somewhere in all that, there's the inherent belief that spending time on getting to the bottom of a problem is 'just a fancy way of doing nothing'.[3]

The very nature of punishment is to make someone suffer by putting them through something unpleasant or painful — the ultimate punishment being the death penalty. But while a punitive response to our children's misdemeanours might work in the short term and serve to modify behaviour, it loses effectiveness over time. Children who are repeatedly punished learn quickly to focus on the avoidance of punishment. They then grow up and often lack the ability to self-regulate. It's as though they've been given an iron exoskeleton that keeps them in check as long as it's in place, but the minute it's removed, they fall apart, go wild, and react strongly to the fetters in which they've been held. We all know those teens who seem to be models of good behaviour in the presence of very strict parents but who then sneak out their bedroom window at night wearing sexy clothes under their pyjamas.

So, the price of enforcing compliance is that it's not really effective over time. It doesn't solve problems; in fact, sometimes it makes them worse. It teaches our children about the use of power and it warps the relationship between the punisher and the punished, impeding any process of ethical development.[4]

If we are always punitive with our children, at home and at school, we raise people who are full of self-pity, rather than human beings who have compassion and empathy for others. We create narcissism rather than altruism. But if punishment is not effective and causes the build-up of stress and the breakdown of relationships, and if letting people get away with everything is not okay, what should we be doing?

Restorative discipline focuses on the idea that the wrong thing causes harm. That is the most important element. Misconduct then is defined as a violation of people and relationships, which in turn creates obligations and liabilities.

Punishment doesn't heal. It doesn't fix things and it certainly doesn't teach our children how they might do things differently. Restorative Practice, on the other hand, seeks to heal and put things right.[5]

If, as parents, we start out by acknowledging when our children do things right, rather than having a mistake-centred approach, we will shape their behaviour. 'Thanks so much for tidying your room' will do a lot more good than, 'It's high time you cleaned up that dump.' *A ratio of four affirmative statements to one negative comment is enough to shape a child's behaviour positively and prevent stress.*

If we're clear about the expectations we have of our children, then it's easy to hold them to agreements. Children don't just *know things*. They need to be told. If we say, 'We're going to see Gran in hospital and there are people there who are not very well, so we need to sit by Gran quietly for a little while and not disturb the others,' we can then gently remind them of our expectations and the reasons for them if they start to get restless and 'misbehave' before the visiting hour is up. We can't assume that children know what to do in each situation, so if we give them the expectations and the reasons, they are much easier to manage. If things do go wrong, we can then talk about what's broken (feelings, relationships or things) and how to fix them.

We have to always maintain our own equilibrium and be firm and fair.

'What are some of the burdens you face as parents?' Margaret asked the group of 25 parents at her restorative parenting workshop.

A mother of a teenage son said, 'My son wants to do whatever he likes. When I tell him he has to be home by 10 p.m., he calls me a control freak. I don't know how to respond to him.'

'Let him know that you may well be a control freak, but that the 10 p.m. curfew is because you want him to be safe. That's your expectation and as long as he lives in your house and you're paying the rent and the food, that's how it is. When he starts contributing financially as an equal, then he can have the freedom that goes along with that.' (It's good for teens to understand that the freedom of adulthood comes along with its responsibilities.)

'My four-and-a-half-year-old won't tidy her room when I tell her to. I tell her she's got fifteen minutes, then I tell her she's got ten, then five, and she still doesn't do it,' said a dad.

'Do you get angry?' asked Margaret.

'Yes, I lose it. I hate losing it,' said the dad.

'So, you can't have a conversation with her when you're angry and she's upset.'

'No,' said the dad. 'I can't talk to her. She just clams up.'

'After you've yelled at her.'

'Right.'

The expectation of this dad, who was doing his utmost to be the best father he could, wasn't in line with his four-year-old's universe. These small human beings do not understand time. Nor can they easily respond to timelines or rational arguments. They can, however, be very capable and compassionate. If that dad goes into his daughter's room and says, 'It's nearly suppertime. Let's clean up together,' and if he sets a great example, there's a really good chance that she will copy him because a) children of this age live in an imitative world, and b) she loves her dad and wants to do things with him. And if he shows gratitude and appreciation for her efforts, he will be modelling for her the behaviour he wants from her.

'I wish I could be more consistent,' said one young mother. 'I go between being completely authoritarian, losing it verbally and being awful, and then feeling guilty and being totally permissive afterwards, allowing my four-year-old to do whatever she wants.'

'I bet your kid has you all figured out,' said Margaret.

As parents, if we stay poised, respectful and calm, we're in the right place to handle the burdens of parenting when they arise. If we're angry, we're better off saying to our offspring, 'I'm too angry to have this conversation right now. Let's talk about it tomorrow.'

In Margaret's family, when someone makes a mistake, the expectation is that the mistake-maker fixes it. When her teenage son called his girlfriend's mobile phone every night for hours on end, the phone bill at the end of the month was double its usual amount. She had a 'restorative chat' with him in which she first asked him what had happened. When he explained the calls, she asked how he thought his dad might have felt when he saw the phone bill. 'Pissed off,' replied her son.

'Right,' said Margaret. 'And how do you think I felt?'

'Pissed off?' he said.

'Yes,' she said. 'What do you think you could do to make things right again?'

'Well, I guess I could pay it back.'

'Good idea,' said Margaret.

Over the next few months he paid back everything. And he never doubled the family phone bill again.

The structure of the restorative chat is such that it can be used in families, in playgrounds, on the street or wherever harm of any kind has been done that needs repair. I have conversations with students along restorative lines several times a week. It is a tool we, as parents and teachers, should all have. It gives everyone a chance to put things right, if and when they do go wrong.

The Restorative Chat

To the person responsible:

- What happened?
- What were you thinking at the time?
- What have you thought about since?
- Who do you think has been affected by what you did?
- In what way?
- What do you need to do to make things right?
- How can we make sure this doesn't happen again?
- What can I do to help you?

To the person affected:

- What did you think when it happened?
- What have you thought about since?
- How has it affected you?
- What's been the worst of it for you?
- What's needed to make things right?
- How can we make sure this doesn't happen again?

When stuck, any or all of these questions
(to the person responsible) can help:

- Was it the right or wrong thing to do?
- Was it fair or unfair?
- What exactly are you sorry for?
- You didn't answer my question.[6]

What we want for our children and how we go about achieving that are sometimes at odds. During the restorative parenting workshop, Margaret asked the group what they wanted for their children. Here are their responses. Parents wanted their children to:

- be happy and contented
- be honest and respectful
- be true to themselves
- be resilient and resourceful
- be compassionate
- be strong and independent thinkers
- be full of humour
- have good self-esteem and self-worth
- be enthusiastic about life, about where they are, about others
- feel purposeful
- get along well with their family
- be curious about the world
- have a love of learning
- be empowered
- be confident
- be good communicators
- be gentle and forgiving of themselves and others.

These parents probably speak for the greater percentage of us no matter where we are in the world. And yet how many of us practise attaining these qualities ourselves and modelling such behaviours in our relationships with our children? After all, as Margaret pointed out, 'If we want our children to be like this, we have to model it.'

We're punitive, grumpy, humourless and angry too much of the time. And the very last thing any parent desires is for their kids to be stressed, unforgiving or violent. Yet all too often, and in numerous ways, we model the very things we wish never to see in them.

Here are the essential aspects of a restorative parenting philosophy:

1. We aim to develop and sustain strong and loving connections that can withstand the ups and downs of family dynamics.

2. We do all we can to promote healthy and positive development of our own and our children's emotional lives.

3. We remain calm in difficult situations without reacting suddenly or emotively.

4. We exercise patience.

5. We take full responsibility for being the adults in the relationship.

6. We're able to manage situations restoratively; everyone involved in the problem is part of the solution.

7. We value relationships above all else.[7]

KEY POINTS

- Restorative parenting prioritises relationships and seeks to repair harm and restore trust. Punishment is not effective in the long term. Children who are repeatedly punished learn to focus primarily on the avoidance of punishment.

- A punitive approach creates narcissism rather than altruism.

- Restorative discipline is based on the principle that the wrong thing causes harm. Misconduct is a violation of people and relationships, which creates obligations and liabilities.

- The restorative chat facilitates accountability in those who have done the harm and allows reparation to be made.

THE PARENT
TOOLBOX

We know now what creates stress. And we know some of the things that can alleviate it and prevent it from becoming a pattern, a state of being, as our children grow. As parents, though, we're often tired and run off our feet and sometimes we just need some helpful hints on how to proceed in the immediacy of the moment, when stress is an unavoidable and already present factor. To that end, in the following chapters, I've outlined the restorative philosophy in more detail and identified some classic 'stress moments' from tots to teens together with some suggestions and examples of responses that can minimise the effects of that stress.

Before moving on to those examples, however, something worth remembering is that parents are not born. We're made. We are formed in the fires of our own learning and struggles, and any true wisdom we acquire is the result of failures and heartbreaks intertwined with success and joy.

Most of us loving, caring parents know intuitively what creates stress in our children and what alleviates it. It's not always easy to practise what we know, though, especially when most of our skills are required in the heat of the moment. And yet, how our relationships with our children develop depends entirely on how we respond to those stressful situations we encounter together.

In the diagram on the following page, developed by Ted Wachtel and Paul McCold at the International Institute of Restorative Practices in Pennsylvania, and adapted by me for this purpose, our parenting styles are set out in small boxes. In the top left-hand corner and the bottom right-hand corner we have what Wachtel describes as 'the punitive/ permissive continuum'. In this model, if we punish, we offer a high degree of control and a low degree of support; if we don't, then we're permissive and we offer a high degree of support and a low degree of control. This is a pretty narrow range and leaves parents with very little room to move.

The punitive and authoritarian parent controls through fear. At the extreme end of authoritarianism we have dictatorships — and we know what that breeds in the civil population. The punitive parent would send the child who doesn't finish cleaning his room to the naughty corner or the bathroom, for 'not doing as he's told'. The permissive parent would make excuses for the child not cleaning his room and do it for him. The result of the permissive parent is a child who then begins to look like a dictator, who 'rules the roost' and does whatever he likes because his parents will always excuse and rescue him.

There are, in fact, other choices. In the bottom left-hand corner there is the neglectful parent, who may be abusive, indifferent or passive in response to children. Neglect can range from benign to criminal, on a sliding scale. The neglectful parent wouldn't care if the child cleaned his room or lived in a dump. If we want to create a low-stress home, we need to look at the top right-hand corner of the diagram. Here is the restorative parent. This parent is supportive and understanding, but firm. This parent holds children *accountable* for their actions but *is also* accountable. At the heart of restorative parenting is the idea that the real currency, the thing that is valued above all else, is *relationship*. And so, no matter what happens, the restorative parent's highest endeavour is *to teach children that relationships are the things we hold in highest regard.*

The restorative parent would work *with* the child and say, 'While you clean your room, I'm going to clean mine. Then in ten minutes we'll call each other in to see how lovely they look.' Or, 'You put the books back in the shelf here and I'll fold your clothes.' Over time, restorative parents make their children more and more accountable and responsible, by modelling the same behaviour.

The four prepositions in the four windows are markers as to how we act. If we're punitive and authoritarian, we stigmatise our children and do things TO them. If we're permissive and undemanding, we do things FOR our children and rescue them from their mistakes. If we're neglectful we do NOT do anything in response to bad behaviour and we're indifferent to what goes on. Finally, if we're restorative, we do things WITH our children and engage them in the process of fixing things or relationships that they have broken. The restorative model puts relationships at the centre of the equation.[8]

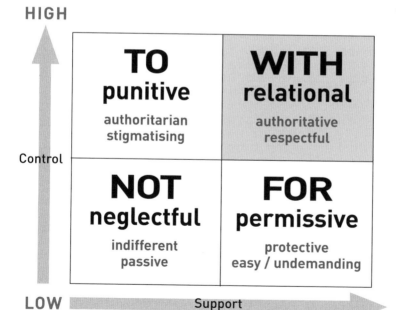

A restorative approach means we always provide our children with the chance to tell their stories and explain what happened. It means we give them the opportunity to be part of fixing things or relationships when they're broken. It means we always provide them with a clear understanding of what we need and expect from them. The restorative chat is a guideline for how we might approach restoring peace when it's been disrupted.

KEY POINTS

- Punitive/Authoritarian parents do things TO their children.

- Permissive/Rescuing parents do things FOR their children.

- Neglectful parents do NOT respond.

- Restorative parents do things WITH their children.

- In restorative philosophy relationships are the real currency.

A BABY'S CRY

For a million different reasons, babies cry. Toddlers cry. We know this means distress. We're often exhausted, sleep deprived and short of patience. No matter what the reason, when infants cry, parents get stressed. That stress pattern is then experienced by the baby, which makes it more difficult for the baby to calm down. When a baby is sick or distressed for any reason, the last thing it needs is for us, as parents, to fall apart. If we shout at each other or at others or, worse, at the baby out of sheer exasperation, we make matters far worse than they already are. The key thing to remember, in those long, long moments while we struggle to find the reason for our baby's distress, is to make ourselves breathe evenly and deeply, and try to bring to mind any thought of gratitude or love. We have to stay calm, remain above the storm.

As we work on our sainthood in this department, we're putting metaphorical money in the bank of our future relationship with our children. A win–win situation. The moment will pass into amnesia one day but the results of our behaviour as parents will have a lasting impact.

If we do manage this trick, not only are we happily on our way to sainthood (defined, in part, by the performance of miracles) but the results are also worth it for everyone. When the baby finally does stop crying, our relationship with our spouse/other children/friends/relatives is still intact, we ourselves have not fallen to pieces, and our baby's nervous system has not been tweaked into the red by our stressful response.

'Oh, he just wants attention,' said a friend of her small baby. Well, absolutely, yes he does! He needs attention. He may need her presence — a lot. Regardless of how inconvenient it is, a *baby* who is screaming needs comfort. He is telling us in the only way he can that he needs us. Remember the Harlow studies and the baby monkey deprived of its mother's loving touch. Nothing good comes from that deprivation. Responding with love to a baby who is screaming is not the same as over-reacting to every whimper and squeak nor is it putting ourselves at the beck and call of a tiny tyrant. We're talking meltdown here, as a result of the most primitive and basic human need: the need to be held, to be comforted. So, we need to stay calm, think beyond the distress and generate an electromagnetic field from our own hearts that is filled with love.

KEY POINTS

- When babies cry, we need to keep our hearts in a loving state.

- Remaining 'above the storm' is worth it for both parents and children.

- Crying babies need our love and attention, even when we're tired.

- The need to be held and comforted is the most basic human requirement.

- Filling our hearts with love as we confront our children's distress pays dividends later.

TEMPER TANTRUMS

The 'terrible twos' sometimes begin at one and sometimes remain until four. Whatever the reason, tots can be overwhelming with their demands, their stubbornness and their reactions when those demands aren't met.

Again, the actual situation is fairly unimportant. It's our *response* that makes or breaks the situation. My husband and I made a decision that diminished stress for us all after a few upsetting incidents. I'm pretty sure every parent under the sun knows this scenario:

- Child throws tantrum.
- Parent A responds to tantrum.
- Parent B responds to Parent A as not doing the right thing/making matters worse and the result is ...
- High stress, or how to achieve complete family dysfunction in five minutes flat.

The practical alternative to this is very simple: we need to understand that a child has a unique and special relationship with each parent, and it's important that we respect our partner's relationship with our child/children.

The course of action that I found to be most helpful and least stressful, and that both my husband and I held to like a life raft, was this: when one of us was dealing with a child who was crying/upset/having a tantrum, the other partner took him/herself out of the fray. (This can work for anyone, assuming at all times that abuse is never part of the picture.) This act, hard as it might seem, results in a far less stressful outcome, as when two stressed people are trying to resolve something, adding a third simply magnifies the problem. The one parent who is left with the screaming toddler (or later, with the sulking teen) can then begin to address the problem restoratively, calmly and even with a touch of humour.

Meltdowns of any kind are stressful on everyone. When faced with a toddler in tantrum/meltdown mode, we're going to exacerbate the problem if we yell or react violently. Our best bet is *never* to stoop to our toddler's level. We have to model the behaviour we want to see. Our relationship with our child is the most important thing.

How many parents have you seen yelling at the tops of their voices, 'STOP YELLING!'? I've seen a lot and I wonder if those parents ever stop to consider the outcome. Can we yell at our kids and then expect them to become suddenly quiet and contrite and say politely, 'Yes, I'm so sorry. I'll be very quiet now …'?

If it's really too noisy, the shutting-yourself-in-a-room trick can be quite effective. Say softly that this noise is hurting your ears and that you need to go into your bedroom for a little while. Try the 'I'll be back out when it's quiet. I love you, and I want to be here with you, but this noise makes my ears hurt' explanation and take note of how you feel when you say it.

Once you've made it to the relative quiet of your room, breathe deeply. You've given your child a boundary without making her feel bad. You still love her, but you have needs too. Wait five minutes — or six, or seven. Then come out and carry on with something else. Those minutes spent in your room have given you a boundary. The incident is over now. Forget the tantrum, even if its dark clouds are still hovering. Confidently, happily, change the focus and your mood, as if you've just gone through a fantastic wormhole at the speed of thought and emerged in a parallel universe where all is well. Ask your toddler to come and plant seedlings with you outside. Children of this age live completely in the moment. When you've left a mood behind, they'll do it easily enough with you.

The break from each other, the change of tack and focus, has a very soothing effect and usually brings stress levels right down for everyone.

Going shopping with small people is always a timed experiment. They will go off at some point and your job is to get through as much as possible, with as much grace as possible, before they start to feel their world unravelling. If, however, the classic scene ensues and a toddler loses it in the shampoo aisle of the grocery store, and is really beyond speech and negotiating, our best bet is to call off the shopping escapade. I mean it. I would take her warmly, lovingly and firmly in both arms and calmly leave the premises. A day without shampoo and milk is worth it. The minute we yell at her or make her feel bad for losing it, we've stooped. We've all done it. I've lived with my own words echoing loudly and mockingly in my ears the day I lost it and bellowed louder than my child, 'You can't just scream and cry every time something doesn't go your way!' Um, yeah, exactly.

A two-year-old will increase the volume of the tantrum in distressed response to a trusted parent losing it too. Of course we're only human, but that thought's hardly comforting when we know that the quality of our relationship with our child depends upon how we maintain our own equilibrium when she loses hers.

We adults set the tone for everything that happens with our young children. They have different behaviours and unique experiences of the world. They are growing, changing beings whose rapid development is the only constant thing about them. They're not, as we so well know, miniature adults. Our responses to their stresses can determine the emotional integrity of our family.

Later on, when relationships are established, it's very, very hard to change the patterns we've established in the early years. But it can still be done. If we, as parents, don't allow ourselves to get stressed or react stressfully, it will have a deep and profound effect on our toddlers. But that requires a degree of wakefulness on our part, otherwise we'll resort to the instinctive reactions that are the results of the unexamined life — those habits we've learned from our own parents or absorbed from the expectations of those around us. We need to *act*, not *react*.

Toddlers need lots of sleep, lots of cuddles and the presence of a loving adult. They need to move and explore. A three-year-old who spends an afternoon opening and slamming his cupboard door is not on a particular mission to irritate. He's exploring movement and airflow. I know this, because I'm the mother of such an experimenter. All children explore their world and want to see how and why things do what they do. Understanding this about toddlers is critical to responding appropriately.

Our children should not be made to feel bad for that exploration but if we respond to their experimenting with annoyance and without understanding what our children are doing, we will place the focus on annoyance. We will create the idea that something is 'wrong' with what a child is doing if we don't properly understand how children need to explore their world. Children will react to our strong emotion that they are not behaving and begin to test that, to see what we will do rather than to see how a hinge on a door works. When that happens, honestly, we've lost the plot and the story of healthy development starts to lose its thread. We've just created an issue where there needn't have been one in the first place.

I was in a paediatrician's waiting room with my sick toddler in Sarasota, Florida, and I watched a young, distraught and tired mother with her sick toddler on another seat. We had both been waiting for the best part of an hour. I attempted to be Entertainment Central in rather depressing surroundings. I sat on the floor, read books, pulled out toys and tried to make the unbelievably slow moments go faster. I was anxious about my child's health but tried to keep my breathing deep and even, though I could tell my son was picking up on my underlying anxiety. I invited toddler number 2 to join us, but her mother kept her firmly on her lap. The little girl was given a pair of car keys, which she began to jangle loudly. Her mother told her to 'shush'. The child ignored the command and kept jangling the keys. The mother said, 'Give me the keys.'

'No!' said the little girl.

The mother grabbed the keys, and put them back into her bag. The frustrated toddler began to scream. The mother yelled. The receptionist looked tense and said, 'It won't be long now.' My child's lip trembled at the distress of a fellow toddler (or maybe because of my stress, who knows?). The mother, at the end of her tether, hauled her child outside where there were more loud and angry words and an increase in the distressed crying. We were now all stressed: my son, me, the receptionist, the mother and her daughter. It was exponential. And ironic: we were all there for the supposed betterment of the children's health!

It's so easy to see, with the clarity of hindsight (or when it's not you), where this situation so often goes wrong. The first error we make is assuming that toddlers are just like us, with all the powers of judgement and logical thought that we have. And with this perspective, someone who jangles keys and keeps doing it when we say 'stop' must be on a deliberate and focused mission to drive us round the bend.

The reality of the situation is light years from this place.

The reality is that the keys are an interesting, moving, shining, clinking, clanging distraction from the monotony of the endless hour in that waiting room.

If that poor, stressed-out mother could have shown interest and joy in the jangling keys, and added a trick or two — shared the perspective of her very little girl — the outcome would have been so completely different. And yet, so often, when we need our powers of imagination and inventiveness the most, we're too tired to find them.

When children say 'no' and begin to assert themselves, they're not refusing our love nor are they questioning our authority. This is the first expression of individuality: our children eventually realise that they're separate beings with their own will. If we meet our obstreperous littlies with humour, distraction and firmness, and if we keep things light, we won't get locked into the situation.

Keeping Things Light is not even on the same continent as Being Permissive. When we're permissive and let them get away with everything or have everything they want, our kids became bossy, insecure and more challenging as they push us to find out where the boundaries are. Children who already have an over-active stress response to the world are worsened by permissive parenting. They need firmness, dependable rhythms to the day and the knowledge that these will be repeated. They need to know that we stand firmly between them and the wide, chaotic world.

The most important thing to remember is that each stressful situation, by itself, is actually pretty unimportant. But how we confront the situation is everything.

So, our five-year-old won't get ready for bed and we've told him twice already. We can shout at him, threaten him, yell at him some more and say, 'NO STORY TONIGHT THEN!' Or we can say, 'Come on, let's get your Thomas the Tank Engine pyjamas out. You put them on, and I'm going to find a very special story for tonight.' We go *with* him into his room. We allow ourselves to feel excited about finding Thomas pyjamas, knowing we have a story about Thomas all lined up. If we're not too tired, we might even make up a story about something that's on our child's pyjamas. That five-year-old is in a world where his imagination reigns supreme. It's a beautiful world. We can be there with him. He won't care that bedtime is at eight whether we threaten him or cajole him. 'Eight' doesn't mean anything. He *will* care about an exciting story and the chance to spend some time with a beloved parent.

I think it's imperative that we learn as parents to focus not on *what* our children have to do but *how* they will be inspired to do it.

I have seen lots of stress at dinner tables in my life, involving children and their eating or not eating, or not eating enough, and I really wonder whether our problems with obesity start with the stress at the table: *Eat your greens! No, you may not leave the table until you've eaten your dinner!* Why is it a problem? A child's sense of taste is extremely sensitive. I would guard against letting the table become a battleground. Kids sometimes cannot handle certain tastes or textures. We ruin this sensitivity early on by giving them sugar and salt and processed foods. Lots of kids are fussy eaters and just refuse certain foods. My take on that is very simple: keep stress away from the table. It's really bad for digestion, and it doesn't take a genius to figure out that creating issues around eating doesn't bode well for a healthy relationship to food.

The stress-free response to a child who won't eat is first and foremost to question. What is it that he won't eat? Is the texture making him gag? Is the taste too intense? Keep children's meals simple. Staying close to nature is important for their health, so if it's beans and broccoli he won't eat, or apples and pears, there are two approaches that in my experience have a high success rate with picky eaters. The best cure is to grow these things ourselves. If a child is involved with picking a few beans and eating them right there in the garden, he will find it incredibly exciting. These things don't have to be eaten at meal times. My son adored tomatoes after we spent time on a friend's farm, hunting for them in the huge veggie garden. They smelled heavenly and earthy at the same time and the taste was magical. Even now, when we buy tomatoes at Woolworths, he'll stick his nose into the packet and say, 'I love that smell.'

The second option is to engage children in the story of their food. One of the most distressing realities is that children in the twenty-first century are often completely disconnected from where food comes from. I've told stories about all kinds of foods to engage children's imaginations in considering the wonderful origins of what they're eating. If we can't grow the stuff and pick it, then we can always tell a great story about *how* it grew and *who* picked it. It's pretty terrifying how many children don't know that milk comes from cows and that potatoes grow underground.

Sometimes children *will* eat things just because the story's good. My son really didn't like quinoa, but I loved it and prepared it for the whole family. I made up a story about a little boy who lived in South America, about the adventures he had and the meals he and his family ate, and how he loved the evenings when the family could finally eat the quinoa they had harvested. When I cooked the grain again when he was older, my son politely declined to eat it. 'Thanks, but I really, *really* don't like the stuff, Ma,' he said. 'You know I just ate it because of that story.' And fair enough. The point is that I'd wanted to connect him to his food.

Involving children in the growing and the cooking of their own food, and helping them to understand food as a wonderful gift from nature, can go a long way to alleviating some of their resistance to certain foods. We have to be sensitive but pragmatic. I've told long stories about how beans grow towards the sun and how yummy sweet potatoes are dug from the ground like treasures. I have managed to 'make' dozens of children eat their greens and I've had a great time doing it. But when they're full, it's imperative to let them stop. We should never use food, or lack of it, as a threat. It should never be a reward or a punishment. Food is life-giving sustenance and we need surprisingly little of the really good stuff to live and be healthy. An attitude of relaxed enjoyment and reverence at the table is the precursor to having no dinner stress.

It's also important for the sanity of the family that we aren't running around stressfully trying to make three different meals for every fussy eater. I've really had to learn to trust that if a child only eats a small amount of what's on the table, because she doesn't or won't eat most of what's on offer, being as nonchalant about it as possible is the best response. I promise that I have used every ounce of self-control to achieve this nonchalance.

So, we make a great meal and we know it's healthy. We know there's something there that most of the family will eat. We need to sit down and enjoy it and not make a big deal out of it if our three-year-old is full after three mouthfuls. She will suffer more from threats and stress than from not eating. What's more, threats and stress are guaranteed to create a problem at the table. Knowing that children are starving around the world does not compute as a valid reason in a child's mind (or mine, for that matter) for needing to wolf down some broccoli.

If we want children to feel gratitude for food and enjoy it, we need to make them intimately part of the process of preparing food. We need them to understand where it comes from, how wonderful it is that this bean needs sunlight and rain and lots of rich soil to grow. Then we won't have to say ever, 'You're lucky to have a meal in front of you. Millions of children your age have no food. You're not leaving the table until you're done.' That, ladies and gents, is a recipe for an eating disorder.

Now back to the grocery-store-meltdown scenario, which is probably one of the most frequently experienced ones, simply because of the sensory overload. Avoiding stress can often be done simply by the art of distraction. A four-year-old has lifted a plastic fire truck from a toy aisle, he has it in his hands and he's not letting it go. Distraction is often the key, and it's all in our voice.

Distraction 1: 'Dad needs a new electric razor and we're going to go and find it now. Come on! We'll wrap it up in special paper when we get home and hide it under his pillow. Let's put the truck back and go get Dad's surprise.'

Distraction 2: 'Tonight I'm going to make a really special fruit salad for everyone. I'd be so happy to let you help me choose the fruit. It'll be a surprise and we won't tell the others what we're going to put in it.'

Sometimes, though, our kids are simply exhausted or physically overwhelmed. No amount of distraction or creative diversion is going to win them over. At this point, our assignment is the same as it always is in situations where nerves are frayed and the heat is rising. We keep our voices low. We breathe deeply. We remain firm and kind and move towards our goal without degenerating into shrieking banshees — I know it's easier said than done, but once it's been done once, it's so much easier to do the second time. We simply pick up our screaming child and make a dash for the haven of the family car.

There is a place for that high-pitched shriek, though: when a child is truly, truly, about to hurt herself if you don't make a really blood-curdling noise. I know that when I raised my voice at my son, it ran like a shockwave through his whole body, terrifying both him and me. When I saw that reaction, I felt the power of an adult's loud voice and I knew that it should be an extremely rare occurrence unless I wanted to create an overactive stress response in my son's small body.

Parents who yell at their kids for running when they should be walking, climbing on the furniture, getting dirty or just doing the normal rough and tumble things that children need to do will create insensitivity and selective hearing, as children act instinctively to protect themselves. Either that, or the yelling will create a nervous condition as the child's sympathetic nervous system is constantly stimulated.

Problems in children's behaviour arise when we use that shriek for *everything.* It loses all its power and eventually our kids numb themselves to their parents' constantly irate, raised voices.

At this age, when children are in an imitative zone, our best bet when dealing with behaviour issues is to engage our children in doing the things we want them to do, with us. When a four-year-old is required to tidy her room, we should get in there and do it with her. Gradually we can let her do more and more of it. If we make a horrible chore of it, by the sound of a nagging frustrated voice or an irritated command, she'll be right in there with us, thinking it's a horrible chore. If we make it a fun but necessary activity, then later, when she's older, she can do it alone.

Meltdowns in little ones require warmth, firmness and consistency from the adults around them. If we show our children that their explosions are storms we can weather with grace, without dissolving ourselves and without giving in to their demands out of sheer exhaustion, they will feel loved and secure.

KEY POINTS

- Don't stoop to the level of the fray.
- Maintain sainthood while the world goes pear-shaped.
- Keep stress away from the dinner table.
- Tell children wonderful stories about where their food came from.
- Children read our emotions much more clearly than they understand our words.
- Keep the high-pitched 'No!' for a truly dangerous moment or it will have no effect when it's really needed.

SIBLING RIVALRIES

When two or more people are gathered together in any kind of a group, there will be issues. Each of us is unique. Our needs are unique. Our responses to the environment and the people in them are unique. The family is a wonderful microcosm of the world community: some people get along just fine, while others drive each other crazy. In the same way, sibling relationships can be harmonious or antagonistic. The most annoying person in a child's world could be her beloved little brother. With little people, issues arise easily. And when we lose our sense of humour and react to these issues as though we're being compelled to prevent World War III, we bring an intensity and stress to things that are really not going to go down in future history books and are instead likely to be forgotten within hours.

Let's talk first about siblings who are not yet at school. As parents, we often take on the role of Supreme Judge in matters of Who-Did-What-to-Whom, but we might easily be inadvertently setting up a rivalry for life by our responses to the spats that siblings get into. The minute we mete out 'punishment' to one sibling, we are on a stress-filled trajectory. Punishment makes our little 'offender' feel shame and does not repair any damage or restore taut relations.

Think restoratively rather than punitively. We do not have to be authoritarian to have authority and we never have to go into the permissive box if we want to be restorative parents. Measured responses to sibling conflicts are essential if we want to keep stress out of the picture and give our relationships the best chance.

It was a late afternoon in Sarasota. We were on the beach with thousands of other families. Near us, six-year-old Jack threw sand in four-year-old Sam's face because Sam had just gleefully stamped on his older brother's sand castle. It is our base instinct as parents, our gut reaction, to protect the smallest and weakest of our offspring at all costs. So, first Jack got slapped (by his mother) for being such a bully to his little brother. When he cried that his sand castle was broken, he was told, 'Your brother's much younger than you. He doesn't understand. We don't throw sand, Jack.' Jack was heartbroken: his sand castle was broken, his arm hurt from the slap, his mother seemed to hate him *and* his little brother was getting all the love and attention.

So, what could that mother have done to restore and repair everything that was broken when one sibling destroyed the other's creation and then got sand thrown in his eyes? The mother might have enlisted Jack's help to get water so that she could wipe the sand out of his brother's eyes. And then, when Sam was all better, she might have enlisted Sam's help to make a new castle for Jack, asking Jack how he might like it to look. Here's an alternative response to a very similar situation, but this one happened years ago, in South Africa.

Matt was four-and-a-half, and Paulie was just two years old. As the two played on the carpet, Paulie broke the wheel of Matt's wooden truck and Matt whacked his brother over the head. Much crying ensued and their mother came into the room. She took both boys in her arms and comforted the crying one. She engaged Matt in kissing and hugging Paulie to make him feel better. 'Let's make him better, Matt. He's very sore.' She sent Matt on an errand to get a bottle for Paulie, which

Matt did with relief, coming back to help his brother. Then she took the broken toy and said to Matt, 'We can fix this, okay? It's not so hard to get the wheels back on.' A little while later, when Paulie had just about forgotten about being hurt, she said, 'Paulie, hold this wheel for Matt. Let's fix the axle.'

It will be evident to these boys, before they can even rationally process it, that both of them are equally loved, that their problems are taken seriously and that relationships matter. Stress has been minimised. For Sam and Jack, on the other hand, it escalated, creating tension in their relationship and in the relationship with their mother.

Now let's talk about slightly older siblings. Jane and Mikel have four children aged seven to twelve. As a full-time primary-school teacher, Jane is as close to superwoman as anyone I've met. She had been teaching for years before she and Mikel had kids and she says, 'I've been a teacher for so long, and you know, no child ever, *ever* got under my skin until I had children. My kids push my buttons and send me to outer space, and that's the thing I've found so confronting.'

Jane and Mikel had an incident with their two youngest boys just the other day where a truly restorative approach helped to avert an emotional catastrophe.

'Jesiah (aged nine) was running out the back door,' Jane says. 'And Roan (five) wanted to follow him. Next thing I knew, someone was crying and Mikel was calling me for help. Outside, Roan was in tears and Jesiah was upset. Here's how the conversation went:

Jesiah: He hit me!

Roan: I didn't!

We had an impasse. I could have just yelled, *Go to your rooms, both of you!* But I didn't. I sat down and took both boys on my lap. Then I looked at my two older children.

Jane: Aiden, were you around?

Aiden: I saw Roan punch Jesiah in the chest.

Jane: Breeagh, did you see anything?

Breeagh: No.

Jane: Roan, did you punch him?

Roan: No!

This process, by the way, took the best part of half an hour. Roan kept interrupting.

Jane: Roany, if you want Mummy to listen to you, wait for your turn. If you keep interrupting, you'll have to go sit in your room.

Jane: Jesiah, what happened?

Jesiah: He punched me in the chest and hit me in the head.

Jane: What happened before that? Was there something you did before he did that?

Jesiah: Yes. I shut the door on Roan.

Jane: How do you think Roan felt?

Jesiah: Sad.

Jane: Thank you so much for telling me that, Jesiah. Thanks for waiting, Roany. Now you tell me what happened.

Roan: I didn't punch him.

Jane: But both Aiden and Jesiah said you punched him. Jesiah, did he actually hit you?

Jesiah: No.

Jane: I see. So, do you know why Roany's sad?

Jesiah: 'Cos I didn't tell the right story.

Jane: Roan, why do you think Jesiah was upset? Might there have been a chance that you touched him?

Roan: Yes, I just touched him. I didn't hit him.

Jane: I'm so proud of you two for being honest. Sometimes if we don't tell the truth, we get a yucky feeling inside. But you know, if you tell, it goes away. Gee I'm proud of you. Roany, how did Jesiah feel about you just touching him?

Roan: He didn't like it.

Jane: So, boys, how do we make it better?

Jesiah: I could say sorry.

Roan: We could play together.

'By this time I was cuddling both of them. This was a real break-through for Jesiah, who feels really bad, really easily. It was big for him to say, "I did do something. I closed the door on him and I told the wrong story." It's really a struggle. I have to work hard to not lose my cool, because my kids press all my emotional buttons and it would be so quick and easy to just send everyone to their rooms. This process took nearly an hour. But next time it won't.'

In this incident, which might look at first like the Spanish Inquisition, it's clear to see that what was actually broken was the relationship and trust between the two boys. And that the most hurtful thing for them was not being understood or heard. The outcome was a true resolution.

These boys are not being primed to play each other for their parents' attention. Nor are they being set up to have an antagonistic relationship with each other. And if something like this happens again, the chances are that they will be more willing to tell the truth and more likely to want to resolve it, because they understand that it will be properly sorted out. They will get the chance to tell their story and they will have the opportunity to repair the harm.

Although it is time consuming to work in this way at first, a reality of life is that building healthy relationships takes time and effort and much love and patience. The rewards, however, last a lifetime.

KEY POINTS

- We don't have to take the role of the Supreme Court.

- Make sure each child feels loved in a situation of conflict.

- Give each child the opportunity to say what they need to say.

- Support honesty.

- Building healthy relationships through restorative parenting takes more time than sending squabblers to their rooms — but the rewards are worth every minute.

FRIENDS AND ENEMIES ON THE PLAYGROUND

For children under seven, intellectual conversations go right over their heads. Imitation, example and an even temperament on our part as parents are what we have to constantly bear in mind. Once children reach the age of about seven the rules change. Now it's possible to engage in conversation when those high-stress moments happen.

While teaching first grade in Sarasota, I was out in the playground with my six- and seven-year-old students. Jakob, always overwhelmingly energetic, had just found a small wooden hammer in the sand pit. Laughingly, he swung it around his head like a helicopter propeller but then the hammer flew out of his hand and hit a little girl, Summer, on the side of her head. I ran over to check on Summer. As I held her to me, I saw blood all over my hand. Quickly, I told the children to wait for me and rushed Summer to the office. In the background I could hear children saying to Jakob, 'You are in big, big trouble.'

In the office, Summer was thoroughly checked over. The hammer had grazed her skin and she was bruised, but she'd sustained a surface injury and within minutes she was all right. I left her in the office just so that staff could keep an eye on her for a while and went back out to the playground.

The mood was tense. Jakob was nowhere to be found.

'He's hiding, Ms Davidow,' Sasha said. 'In the bushes.'

She pointed and I went to find Jakob. I could sense everyone's eyes on me. How I dealt with this would determine what kind of an adult I was and what these children could expect from me. The fear was palpable as I located Jakob and asked him to come out of the bushes. He was shaking and crying.

'Come and sit down next to me and tell me what happened,' I began.

He sobbed and tried to recount the incident. 'I didn't mean for the hammer to hit Summer, I really didn't.'

'I understand,' I said.

'I won't ever, ever do it again,' he said, sobbing.

'Did you see her head was bleeding?'

He nodded.

'What did you think when you saw what happened?'

He wanted to know if she was going to live.

'She's hurt, but she's going to be okay. She'll have a bump where the hammer hit her.'

'I'm really sorry. It just flew out of my hand.'

'So, do you think you know a few things about hammers now? Even toy hammers?'

He nodded vigorously. 'Don't swing them around.'

'Right,' I said.

'Can I see Summer?'

'In a little bit. She'll be back in class when she feels better.'

The next day, Summer came to school with a smile on her face and a small bump on the side of her forehead. Jakob ran to her to ask if she was okay. He apologised. The day went on as usual. At a certain point in time the children were allowed to do a drawing of anything they liked. Jakob didn't know what to draw. He sighed and complained loudly.

'I know, Jakob,' Summer said, 'why don't you draw *you* throwing the hammer and it hitting *me* on the head.' She grinned.

'Yeah!' he said. They proceeded to discuss exactly what had to be in the picture. Summer was sitting behind Jakob, so the conversation was tricky.

'Ms Davidow, can I sit next to Jakob?' Summer asked.

'Yes,' I said. 'Just bring your chair over to his desk.'

I watched the children as they chatted and laughed. Soon others were offering ideas for what needed to go into Jakob's picture. The situation was completely resolved, but I saw that it was actually *more* than resolved. It was entirely transformed. Relationships weren't only intact; they were deeper. Everyone had learned something. There had been pain and tears and remorse, and what Jakob went through in the bushes as he pondered the disaster that he'd just caused was certainly 'punishment' for his inadvertent 'crime'.

That situation was the beginning of a relationship between my class and me based on trust. From that incident they understood that there were consequences and responsibilities when things went wrong, as opposed to punishments. An important and subtle aspect to this was that the children understood that there was no adult venom attached to these consequences.

Our agreement was that if you broke something or hurt someone or did something that caused others any kind of pain, you had the opportunity to fix it. That was all.

Restorative approaches can work in almost any situation where harm has been done by someone and needs to be fixed. When children hurt each other or don't do as they're asked or are rude or misbehave in any way, our first approach has to be one where we rise above the storm. Then, as we negotiate the road to resolution, repairing the harm, we keep within our sights what we ultimately want for our children.

KEY POINTS

- The focus in any incident should be on what harm has been done and how it can be healed.

- There is no blame and no shame.

- Sometimes the 'crime' is already punishment.

- Handling things restoratively is not a soft option.

- Accountability is much healthier than guilt.

DEALING WITH BULLIES

There's nothing quite so stressful for us as parents than hearing about or witnessing our children being bullied. There are many books devoted to the subject of bullying, and it's beyond the scope of this one to go into it in detail, but suffice it to say that acts of bullying are a worldwide phenomenon. They affect millions of people and result in untold stress, heartache and, yes, suicides. If your child is being bullied, the very last thing he needs is to be told to toughen up and face it or to ignore it. He also doesn't need a furious parent to rush in and attempt to 'solve' the problem. These tactics backfire.

What, then, is the answer when we're witnessing bullying going on in front of us and all we really want to do is rush in and tear the bully limb from limb?

The only truly effective strategy that I can say I have confidently used is the restorative chat. It's objective, it's without blame and it ensures awareness of the problem in the minds of the people doing the bullying. It can be used at a moment's notice with our own children or with complete strangers and it is geared to repair harm.

Here's an example of a restorative chat I had with some twelve-year-olds on the playground after a boy called a girl a slut as she walked by and I happened to be on duty and within earshot.

'Tom, just come here a minute, please. You, too, Jen. Tom, I just heard you call Jen a slut. Do you know what a slut is?'

Tom shrugged.

'A slut is someone who sleeps around. What were you thinking when you called Jen a slut?'

'I dunno. I wanted to annoy her.'

'Tom, how do you think your words affected Jen?'

'Badly, I guess.'

'Jen, what's the worst of this for you?'

'It hurts me a lot. I get called names often. By Tom, but not only him. I'm thinking of leaving the school. I just want to be left alone.'

'Tom, what do you need to do to make things right for Jen, so that she doesn't have to feel this bad?'

'Stop calling her names and stuff.'

'Jen, what do you need from Tom in order to make things right here?'

'I just want him and his friends to mind their own business and leave me alone. I don't go bothering them and I think they should find something better to do.'

'Tom, does this seem like a fair request?'

'Yes.'

'Is there something you'd like to say to Jen?'

'I'm sorry for calling you names. I'll leave you alone and won't bother you anymore.'

'How will you make sure this doesn't happen again?'

'I'll stop and tell my friends to stop.'

'Tom, I will hold you to that. In three weeks' time, at the end of term, I will check in with Jen and with you and make sure that you've held to your agreement.'

That was the end of the matter. The conversation took less than five minutes. Jen and Tom certainly weren't the best of friends afterwards, but when I checked in with both of them (separately) at the end of the term, it was as if the incident had never taken place. Jen said she was fine, was not being bothered by Tom or his friends anymore and didn't remember having said she'd wanted to leave the school.

I have about three such conversations every week. Sometimes the incidents are physical (punching, kicking, etc.), but very rarely. Once in a while a serious conference with several sets of parents and teachers is required. Mostly, the harm children do to one another is psychological. And when that's serious, and if even a single adult is aware of the problem, a full conference is necessary. The best way to end the cycle that drives so many young people to depression and sometimes to the edge of desperation is to address the harm head on and allow the bullies to stand in the shoes of the bullied and feel their pain. The restorative solution is delicately constructed and carefully controlled. Using Restorative Practice reduces incidents of bullying radically in schools and it is being implemented all over the world in a wide variety of settings. Knowing even just the basics of the restorative chat, is, as I've mentioned, one of the most valuable tools we can have in our kits.

Here are some key points that we might take on board as essential foundations on which we can rely as we face the many rocky challenges of parenting our children in a low-stress way:

1. **Foster awareness:** Children need to know how their actions impact others around them. If children do something wrong, we can tell them how it feels for us as parents or we can get the affected sibling/friend to explain what it feels like for them.

2. **Avoid scolding or lecturing:** We want our children to feel empathy, not guilt. Guilt makes them feel like victims themselves and detracts from the real issue

at hand. Empathy allows them to focus on the person who's been affected.

3. **Involve children actively:** Children need to be part of the process of repairing the harm done. They need to be able to offer ideas on how they plan to make amends. This holds them accountable.

4. **Accept ambiguity:** Sometimes it's impossible to tell who started the fight/broke the toy/etc. Encourage children to take as much responsibility as they can, and continue to work out a solution where everyone offers a plan to make amends.

5. **Separate the deed from the doer:** Be clear that it's not Kirsty that's the problem. It's her *behaviour* and its effect on those around her. We could say, 'I know you had no idea how this was going to impact Rachel ...' or, 'I know that usually you're very sensitive towards others, Kirsty ...' It's fine to love the child and really not love the behaviour.

6. **See every instance of wrongdoing or conflict as an opportunity for growth and learning:** From experience, let me say that we can use every conflict and behaviour issue as an opportunity to build empathy, deepen relationships and our sense of community, and reduce the likelihood of the same thing happening again.[9]

KEY POINTS

- Bullies need to know how their actions impact others.

- Bullies need to be given the opportunity to experience empathy.

- The behaviour needs to be seen as separate from the person.

- Bullies need to be actively involved in healing the harm.

- We need to see conflict as an opportunity for everyone to grow.

INDEPENDENT
TEENS

Your sweet, tree-climbing and studious bookworm suddenly turns into the next supermodel and buries herself under acres of mascara and lip gloss. Your mischievous swimming champ suddenly turns a different colour, stops kissing you and becomes the Incredible Hulk overnight. Vaguely, in their faces, you see flickers of personality reminding you that these are, in fact, your children.

It's not always that dramatic but, compared to who they were when they were eleven, teenagers are a different species. And parenting takes on a whole new world of meaning!

If we haven't established a home with firm boundaries and warm relationships based on trust and love, then dealing with teens is a very tricky business and the risk of alienating them is high. Teen brains are going through that rapid global pruning process we described in earlier chapters. Specific skills are being honed. The most used neural networks remain and the least used are pruned. Our neural patterning as adults is a result of this pruning process, so it's good to remind ourselves that what our children are doing for the majority of their time is of real significance to their neurological development.

The human brain takes our entire childhood to mature. It is the last part of our anatomy to reach maturity. That should tell us everything we need to know about how we deal with our children. Significantly, too, the last part of the brain to reach maturity is the prefrontal cortex, especially the dorsolateral prefrontal cortex which is important in gauging social norms. As mentioned earlier, it's where we process the idea of *consequences* for our actions. This part of the brain is not fully mature until around the age of 21. Judging social norms and expectations is a very delicate and complex process involving both the emotional and rational centres of the brain. And if the emotional centre of the brain develops faster than the rational centre, it's not hard to see how difficult it can be, even when teens are not stressed, for them to gauge the consequences and possible outcomes that would result from certain behaviours.

Our children go from being interested in certain foods and averse to others (simple sympathies and antipathies) when they're young, to being interested in being approved of, and averse to being shunned, by a social peer group when they're teens. It's a whole shift in priorities and, as I well remember, not an easy place to be.

Being the parent of a teenager has certain similarities with being the parent of a toddler. But the marked difference is that our teens *do* have the capacity to have quite in-depth conversations and to reason (even if this reasoning sometimes comes after the fact!). They can relate to us in a way that two-year-olds can't. We can have adult discussions.

For those living with tots or teens, the metaphor of still waters suddenly becoming wild tidal waves is a valid one. Our teens are not yet adults. Their brains are going through some rapid sculpting and their bodies are at the mercy of raging hormones. Yet there are times when they are so very adult, so logical and insightful and quite brilliant. They are angelic and adorable and admirable one moment, and out of control and furious and frustrating the next. And we have to keep on loving them through it all, just as we did when they were two.

At this point, we have to elegantly step from being the loving *authority* in their lives to being the wise *advisor* with inner authority, available to guide and support.

We can pick up a tired, crying two-year-old and tuck her into bed.

We can't pick up a tired, crying fourteen-year-old and tuck her into bed.

In fact, we cannot actually *make* our teens do anything. Which is why I see many parents resorting to extreme forms of behaviour management that end up firmly in the punitive department. Teens are threatened, bribed, cajoled, grounded and relieved of certain privileges on a grand scale. I understand the desperation. The last thing we want to feel is that we've lost control. But the reality is that we are not in control. Now is the time when we are most tempted to slip into the punitive/permissive box. Instead, we have to rely on the fact that they are thinking, feeling human beings who have the capacity for *empathy* and we should not have to resort regularly to threats, bribes and punitive measures to keep our teens safe and behaving respectfully towards us.

So, what can we do when emotions run high and the opportunity for stressful situations is magnified to gigantic proportions in our families?

We should make some time to sit with our children to talk about how we go about creating an optimum home environment. If we outline our expectations and come to an agreement *together* about how to make things work, it's much easier to deal with issues when they do come up. Expectations need to be explicit. Assume nothing.

Here's an example of a family conference with a parent and two teens to establish a low-stress, happy home, based on restorative philosophy and several real conversations.

Parent: Okay guys, we're here to talk about how we create a *well-functioning* home environment where we all *enjoy* being in the same house, where we *understand each other's needs* and *share* the things that need to be done so that it's fair. So, first of all, I'm assuming that we want to live in a home that's a happy, stress-free place, where everyone feels respected, where everyone does their bit to help; a home where, when things or trust are broken, we focus on how to repair them. Does that sound fair enough?

The kids (let's call them Max and Fiona) should nod, unless they're channelling a demon, in which case, rephrase the question until they get real.

Parent: So, what are some of the things we can do to make this home environment work well?

(Lots of suggestions should emerge here. Always bring the focus back to the original plan: the goal is a well-functioning, happy, stress-free place where everyone is respected and does their bit to help, and where things or relationships are fixed when broken.)

Parent: That all sounds great. I do love the suggestion that everyone needs to take turns with cleaning up after dinner. And the idea that one person can request another to not go into their room unless they ask is also a fair one. Thanks for that input. Okay, I'm going to tell you guys what I need from you so that my parenting job is less stressful, after which you'll have a turn to express what you need. So, firstly, I need you to confine your mess to your rooms. If it spills out all over the house, or if things start living and growing in there and becoming a health hazard for the rest of us, I'm going to request a clean-up. Does that seem fair?

Max and Fiona: Sure.

Parent: Also, I need you to limit your entertainment screen time so that it's within a healthy range. If it's more than 20 hours a week, you're in the danger zone and I'm going to turn into the protective lioness and stop you doing it, so you must keep conscious of that. I need everyone to assist with the other household stuff, like folding laundry and taking out the rubbish, so that I don't feel like the maid when I get home from work. Does that seem fair to you?

(Obviously other parents' lists will look a little different.)

Max and Fiona: Yes.

Parent: Okay, great. So, if I need to remind you about it, I will. So now tell me what your needs are in order for us all to have a well-functioning and low-stress home.

(We need to be prepared to really listen, and guide things back to what our family objective is here.)

Fiona: I need you to not keep getting on my back about my homework. I do always do it and it makes me stressed when you keep asking me.

Parent: That sounds fair.

Max: When you ask me to do something, it often sounds like I've got no choice, so more like I'm being told. I want to be asked so that I feel I'm being respected, and that if I say okay I'm not doing it because I'm told.

Parent: I'll take that to heart.

Fiona: I hate being rushed in the morning, and when people call me names it puts me in a bad mood.

Parent: So, if you're not ready and it's getting late and the rest of us are ready to go, what's your suggestion for a low-stress alternative?

Fiona: Just tell me quietly and not angrily when there's fifteen minutes to go until we leave. I don't want to be called names by Max first thing in the morning. I just want it to be calm.

Parent: That sounds like a fair request. Can I ask that you take the responsibility for getting yourself to the car on time?

Fiona: Yes.

Parent: Okay, the only thing I'll say is, *fifteen minutes till departure.* Let's see how that goes. Max, does it sound fair that you stop calling her names?

Max: Yes.

Parent: Great, guys. So, can we agree that we'll work with each other to make sure those needs are met? If we go off-track at any time, we'll come together and, without blame, we'll see what needs fixing and how we do that.

That discussion is there as scaffolding when things do go awry, which, with teens, they will sometimes do.

In the game of Real Life, we are the ones with the experience and the wisdom. Our teens might want to share things about their world with us, but we're often too busy, too involved in our own lives, to take much notice. We *need* to take notice.

If our teens feel understood, if we acknowledge *their* body of knowledge with genuine interest, they are at much less risk of following that teen trajectory of feeling grossly misunderstood, generally becoming deeply stressed and distressed or developing suicidal tendencies.

Lisa is a councillor and the mother of three teens. She told me about a recent impromptu family 'conference' she held, restorative style, in the middle of a forest in the middle of a holiday hike, to stop a potential issue before it had the chance to ruin things.

Her eldest teen, Jeremy (nineteen), had been 'throwing a few put downs his younger sibling's way'. Lisa's husband Rick grew increasingly angry and told Jeremy off quite harshly. Lisa says, 'Everyone went quiet and the tension in the air threatened to hijack the holiday. I called the whole family to a nearby picnic area and explained to everyone that we were all going to say how we were feeling and what we thought about things ... I asked everyone to not interrupt and listen to everyone's experience. I started. I named the behaviour, the anger and the silence and my aspirations for the holiday. My eldest got to hear how everyone experienced his banter, even though he had not intended it to be hurtful. My husband got to hear how his angry outburst made things worse. My youngest, Ben (fifteen), finished by saying he just wanted us all to have a happy holiday. It was enough. The air was cleared and we went on to have one of our favourite family holidays.'

In another incident, Lisa had a restorative chat with Ben, after she'd heard that he and a group of friends had been smoking at a recent party. 'When I questioned Ben, he was silent and would not admit involvement. I lowered my voice to a whisper and proceeded to ask him what he was thinking at the time. He opened up and so I asked him what he'd thought about since the incident and who he thought might have been affected. He didn't know. I suggested that his friends' parents were upset and their trust had been affected, as had ours. Even though he was being open and honest, when I pressed for where the cigarettes came from, he clearly told me he would not dob in a mate. I accepted this. Then I asked him what he could do to make things right. He apologised to me. We decided together that he would write a letter to his mates' parents apologising and acknowledging what had happened. We sent the letter and he later remarked how pleased he was that he did it. It enabled him to feel comfortable around those parents again.'

Lisa explains how important it is to allow teens to learn their lesson without lecturing them on top of it. When Jeremy first got his licence, he drove way too fast and, as any parents would, Lisa and Rick cautioned him and 'pep-talked ourselves stupid. All it achieved was Jeremy's denial and defensiveness. We even had friends comment on his fast driving! We were left to worry and pray.'

A few months later, at night, they got a call that Jeremy had been in an accident. He was okay but had crashed into the back of another car. 'As I arrived at the accident scene I was met by the (furious) mother of the other new driver. She told me she'd called the police and tow trucks. My son was sitting alone in the back of our open stationwagon. All our fears had been confirmed. I was tempted to lecture the lesson to him. Instead, I took a deep breath and crawled in beside him. I asked him if he was okay and to tell me what had happened. My son acknowledged he was driving too fast on a dirt road.

'The other mother was furious with Jeremy, which was why he had crept into the back of the car. She'd told him she was going to make sure he was penalised. The police, however, did not penalise him. It was the other driver's third accident!'

Lisa did not have to say anything to Jeremy. 'The tow trucks arrived; my son paid for the towing and we went home. The next week was busy for him, making calls, getting quotes, dealing with insurance companies and the mother. We guided him through the whole process but insisted he do it himself. The towing and excess depleted all his savings … even though we were insured.

'There was very little talk about it. Our relationship stayed intact. He'd learnt his lesson and slowed down. Most importantly, we know that he will always know it is safe to call on us in times of crisis, no matter what.'

Teens argue with their parents about many things. It's their job. And we know they rebel and do crazy things and are rude as they work out who they are in the world and how they are unique. They need to push away from us to some degree to delineate who *they* are. It doesn't mean they don't love us anymore. Having restorative chats and even conferences is a very effective way to avoid stress and to enable transformation with our teens in times of conflict, as their brains slowly reach full maturity.

The following scenario, with its less than happy outcome, occurred recently at our school, but similar situations could equally happen in any family. Rumour had it that certain high-school boys were smoking illegal substances in the bushes at school. The boys denied it. Then they said okay, they were smoking, but only regular tobacco. Nevertheless, a marijuana plant was found growing close to where the boys had smoked. It was taken and destroyed.

Under 'normal' circumstances, the police would be notified and punishment of one kind or another (suspension, expulsion, being charged with possession of illegal substances) would ensue. This was the first time anything like this had taken place in our high school. We called in the parents and the boys and one other teacher. The focus of the meeting was to understand what harm had been done and then see what could be done to repair the damage.

In this case, trust and even possibly the law had been broken.

I was the facilitator at this conference. We stated what had happened and asked the boys what they were thinking when they went off and smoked in the bushes.

'I dunno,' one said. 'It was fun.'

'Yeah, exciting,' said another.

'What have you thought about since then?' I asked, following restorative conference etiquette.

'It was probably stupid,' said one.

I asked the parents how it had affected them.

'I'm horrified that you'd do something like this,' one dad said to his son. 'School's a public place. I'm shocked that after all we've talked about you can put yourself and others in such a situation. If you break rules that are there for your own safety and the safety of others in a public domain, no one can protect you. It's really hard on me,' said the dad.

That went to his son's heart. He was close to tears.

'What's been the worst of it for you?' I asked a mother.

'Loss of trust,' she said. 'It's pretty terrifying to me to think that I can't trust my own kid.'

I asked the teacher how it had affected him.

'Well, like your dad said,' he said, referring to the one boy, 'if you break the law at school, I can't protect you, your parents can't protect you. I lose trust and the whole school community hears about it and we get rumours, a bad name. Some parents might pull their kids out … It's like starting a fire when the wind is high. It affects the whole school. The community.'

The boys were distressed. I asked the parents and teacher what they needed in order to feel trust again. Of course they needed absolute assurance from the boys that this wouldn't happen again.

What moved these boys to the point of tears was losing their parents' trust. In particular, seeing their dads so upset was very disturbing for them.

'If the police get involved,' said one dad, 'then no amount of talk is going to change anything. If you want to smoke and experiment, do me a favour: don't do it in a public place and put so much at risk. Talk to me about it. I was young once, you know.'

After more than an hour, the conference ended with an apology from the boys to their parents and teachers. There were lots of tears and hugs between fathers and sons. A written agreement was signed by everyone present that the boys would refrain from these risk-taking behaviours. The parents of the boys also required that for the next month their sons would be home every evening by 7 p.m., and that they be home on the weekends. Re-establishing family balance and integrity was essential to them.

We had hoped that this would be the end of that matter, but not every story has a happy ending. One year later, one of the same boys was caught doing the same thing again. Because he had broken his agreement, and the basis of trust was now completely eroded, he was suspended from school for the upcoming semester. He chose not to return. He'd had the chance to come clean, but now had to face the consequences of the decision (and it was his decision) to continue breaking rules that were there for everyone's safety.

In another scenario, a sixteen-year-old boy who had already left the school came back over the holidays with some friends, broke into a classroom, released the fire extinguisher and caused hundreds of dollars worth of damage and untold inconvenience and distress to members of the school community. The culprit was discovered through Facebook conversations that led to chats that parents overheard. He and his friends were given the opportunity to participate in a restorative conference.

The police still charged the teens, but those who participated in the conference were able to apologise, to come back and clean up, fix and restore the classroom to order. Most importantly, they had the opportunity to hear how their actions had affected others, to restore their dignity and standing in the community. We overlook this aspect almost entirely as a society when we go about punishing and labelling the troublemakers. This act, which allows teens to 'save face', is essential for their emotional health.

And then they had to face the reality that they each, now, had a police record.

But those are big issues. What about small, everyday misdemeanours? Many of the elements that create a low-stress family environment are the same for teens as they are for the tiniest babies. As parents we have to stay calm and maintain saint-like breathing, even while an inner dragon is starting to form just beneath the surface of our skin. Remember that generating a highly coherent heart-rhythm pattern can have an actual effect on the heart rhythms of someone near us. So, if a teen is simply rude and obnoxious or not listening and we are over it, we should not give in to our immediate response to want to do the same right back or get really defensive.

If we succumb, the result will be high stress. I've done it and, to be honest, I can't see any benefits.

Instead, we need to fasten our seatbelts.

'I hate you!' sixteen-year-old Ella shrieks. 'You never listen to me and you never let me do what I want! Kian always gets what he wants.'

That moment right there is too hot to handle. I wouldn't touch it (now that I'm older and wiser). I've done it before and got burned. The best response, in my experience, would be, 'Ella, I hear you and I really want to talk about that, but I'm too hurt right now, and you're too angry.'

Later, maybe even the next day, we can have a real conversation. I've had several of these. Here's an example of how this scenario could play out beneficially.

'Hey, Ella, let's talk about when you say you hate me and I never listen. Tell me about that.'

Then we have to let her tell. (It does take sainthood and a lot of guts. We have to be prepared to *really* listen.)

'So, Ella, I've heard you and I'll come back to you on all those things. But first just hear things from my point of view. It's totally heartbreaking to hear the person I love more than my own life tell me that she hates me. Everything I do is with your best interests at heart, and sometimes, for sure, I'm clumsy and make mistakes. You're right, I'm sometimes distracted and don't listen. I'm going to do my best to really change that. I do try to be fair and give you and Kian everything in equal measure. Sometimes, though, because he's older and has already had the opportunity to show me he's responsible, I do allow him more freedom. Freedom, though, comes with responsibility. He's a safe driver, he's always home when I ask him to be home and I trust him. When I know your friends and trust them that much, you can also go out with them and come back later.'

'You won't even give me the chance to show you I'm responsible.'

'All right, let's make a decision then about how you can do that.'

And when we make that decision, we need to follow through on it. There will be less of a disconnect, less chance of a recurrence of a violent verbal outbreak.

And in keeping with the restorative philosophy, we can tell our teens that it's really important that they understand how their words impact us. It's most likely they'll apologise and hug us, especially if we've given them a genuinely good example of how to apologise with grace — especially if we've admitted we've made a mistake too.

It's always beneficial to teens to see that the adults around them are human. And that they can be humble. It's important we don't whine and get accusatory and make them feel bad, because they'll just do that right back to us. And we know how that feels.

Recently when one of my classes had a very feral day, I went home and felt like getting in my car and driving north indefinitely.

I returned, despite my better judgement, the next day. 'Year Sevens,' I said, 'you're a great group of people and I really enjoy teaching you. Yesterday, though, you were so wild and noisy that I had a very hard time teaching you. I couldn't get anything done that I really wanted to do and, ultimately, that was your loss as well as mine. Let's remind each other of the qualities we need to demonstrate in order for this learning environment to be fun and beneficial to everyone.'

We went through all the things we'd agreed needed to be in place at the beginning of the year to have a really healthy learning environment: respect for others, quiet when someone else is speaking, etc.

'Can we please have a different mood in here today?'

They agreed, we had a much better day, and I was no longer planning how quickly I could drive north.

Teens have the capacity to do things that put parents' teeth on edge. They may drive too fast. They may use the computer inappropriately. They may experiment with drugs and take social and sexual risks. They will keep secrets from us and sleep late and their rooms will look like the aftermath of a clothing-factory explosion. And they won't always do what we tell them to do — especially if we don't treat them with the respect we require *from* them. And we will seriously wonder whether our own child has been abducted by aliens and replaced by a foreign entity, a changeling who bears a striking resemblance to someone we love more than anything.

By this point, perhaps some of the reasons things are the way they are have become clearer. And with the knowledge we have, we can respond so that we end up with deeper connections with the children we love than we ever had before. All the work we do in our children's early years will pay off somewhere here, when some of the biggest challenges come to meet us.

KEY POINTS

- Be explicit about expectations and needs.

- Don't be defensive and accusatory.

- Don't lose sight of what really matters.

- Get the family off the stress highway.

- Be more actively loving.

FINAL
THOUGHTS

If we want the next generation to live longer, happier lives and contribute to a better world because of it, it's our assignment as parents to be less stressed, more conscious and more actively loving. It's time we all made a graceful and speedy exit off the stress highway ... the one we often don't even know we're on. This crazy road towards a glaring finishing line of necessary distinctions and achievements is one of the most unacknowledged, unexamined and devastating concepts stressfully impacting our children today.

Likewise, reactive and often punitive or permissive parenting, the onslaught of disturbing media, the disconnect experienced because our children's social lives are so media-saturated, and schools that are often more closely related to correctional institutes than educational ones, leave young hearts ill at ease. As parents who are members of a global community responsible for how the next generation will develop, we have an incredible opportunity to work with the enormous amounts of information available to us and to positively transform the way we are, the things we do and, consequently, the adults our children will become.

If we parents in our billions could live our lives filled with love and with informed awareness for how our children are developing, who knows? We might live to see a decrease in heart disease, teen suicide and other stress-related illnesses that are currently epidemics of considerable proportions.

Childhood and adolescence is an all-too-brief time in which we can give our children the tools that they will need to cope in the world. If we tip the scales, redress the imbalance between fear and love in *our own lives*, we have the most precious opportunity to help our children become the healthy, happy, successful and fulfilled adults of tomorrow that they deserve to be.

ACKNOWLEDGEMENTS

I'm deeply grateful to Professor Rollin McCraty at the Institute of HeartMath in California for his enormous generosity, expertise and insight. Thanks to David Poff, MD, of Australia's Royal Flying Doctor Service for lending an essential critical medical eye to the first draft of this manuscript; to neuroscientist Paul Liknaitzky, for answering complicated late-night questions; to therapist David Garb for his wisdom; to Jane Blomkamp, Liz Blomkamp, Anouska Jones, Tracy Griffiths and Nicole Swartz, mothers extraordinaire, thank you for sharing your stories; to George McWilliam for valued insights on 'The Right Thing at the Right Time'; to my students and colleagues; and my parents and siblings for teaching me so much; and to the wonderful team at Exisle Publishing whose ethos makes the world a better place.

NOTES

Introduction

1. World Health Organization, Fact sheet no. 317, January 2011, <http://www.who.int/mediacentre/factsheets/fs317/en/index.html>

2. Smith, Rebecca, 'Stress Increases Risk of Death Fivefold', *Daily Telegraph*, 2010, <http://www.telegraph.co.uk/health/healthnews/7991620/Stress-increases-risk-of-death-five-fold.html>

3. Chandola, T., 'Chronic Stress at Work and the Metabolic Syndrome: Prospective study', *British Medical Journal*, 2006, vol. 332, pp. 7540

4. Fairtest, *Wales Drops Most Standardised Testing*, <http://www.fairtest.org/wales-drops-most-standardized-testing>

5. O'Keefe, Darah, *NAPLAN Nightmare*, 2011, <http://www.maggiedent.com/content/naplan-nightmare-%E2%80%94-education-review-article>

6. Stewart, Francis, 'School Tests Harming Kids', 2012, <http://www.canberratimes.com.au/act-news/school-tests-harming-kids-20120303-1ua26.html#ixzz1zXNM3O1N>

7. *Measures of Australia's Progress*, 2010, <http://www.abs.gov.au/ausstats/abs@.nsf/Lookup/by%20Subject/1370.0~2010~Chapter~Mental%20health%20(4.1.6.7)>

8. Uk.answers, 'How can I cope with school stress (GCSEs)?', 2009, accessed July 2011, <http://uk.answers.yahoo.com/question/index?qid=20100303120217AAGxz6U>

9. Smith, L., *World Socialist Website*, 2004, accessed 11 July 2011, <http://www.wsws.org/index.shtl>

10. UNICEF, 'Child Poverty in Perspective: An overview of child wellbeing in rich countries', *Innocenti Report Card 7*, UNICEF Innocenti Research Centre, Florence, 2007

Part One: Stress

1. Sapolsky, Robert, *Why Zebras Don't Get Ulcers*, Owl Books, New York, 2004

2. McCraty, Rollin, Mike Atkinson and Dana Tomasino, *Science of the Heart: Exploring the role of the heart in human performance*, Institute of HeartMath, California, 2007

3. ibid.

4. ibid.

5. ibid.

6. McCraty, Rollin, Mike Atkinson, Dana Tomasino, and Raymond Trevor Bradley, *The Coherent Heart: Heart–brain neurological interactions, cognitive performance, and the emergence of system-wide order*, Institute of HeartMath, California, 2004

7. McCraty, Rollin, Mike Atkinson and Dana Tomasino, *Science of the Heart: Exploring the role of the heart in human performance*, Institute of HeartMath, California, 2007

8. ibid.

9. Damasio, Antonio, *Looking for Spinoza*, Harcourt Inc., New York, 2003

Part Two: Environments

1. Goldberg, Wendy A., Granger, Douglas A., Middlemiss, Wendy, Nathans, Laura, 'Asynchrony of Mother–Infant Hypothalamic–Pituitary–Adrenal Axis Activity Following Extinction of Infant Crying Responses Induced During the Transition to Sleep', *Early Human Development*, 2012, vol. 88, Issue 4, pp. 227–32

2. 'Babies Left to Cry "Feel Stressed" ', *Daily Mail*, 23 September 2012

3. *Children's Health and the Environment*, <http://www.who.int/ceh>

4. Harlow, H., *Psych Classics*, 2011, retrieved 3 June 2011, <http://psychclassics.yorku.ca/ Harlow/fig4jpg>

5. ibid.

6. Harrison, Linda Law, 'The Use of Comforting Touch and Massage to Reduce Stress in Preterm Infants in the Neonatal Intensive Care Unit', *Newborn and Infant Nursing Reviews*, 2001, vol. 1, no. 4 (December), pp. 235–41

7. McCraty, Rollin, William A. Tiller and Mike Atkinson, 'Proceedings of

the Brain–Mind Applied Neurophysiology EEG Neurofeedback Meeting', Key West, Florida, 1996

8. Pribram, Karl and Deborah Rozman, 'Early Childhood Development and Learning: What New Research on the Heart and Brain Tells Us about Our Youngest Children', White House Conference on Early Childhood Development and Learning, 1994

9. ibid.

10. McCraty, Rollin, Mike Atkinson and Dana Tomasino, *Science of the Heart: Exploring the role of the heart in human performance,* Institute of HeartMath, California, 2007

11. McCraty, Rollin, 'The Psychophysiology of Positive Emotions and Optimal Functioning', *The Appreciative Heart*, Institute of HeartMath, California, 2003, and McCraty, Rollin, 'The Heart as a Hormonal Gland', 2003, <http://www.heartmath.org/research/science-of-the-heart/soh_6.html>

12. McCraty, Rollin, Mike Atkinson and Dana Tomasino, *Science of the Heart: Exploring the role of the heart in human performance,* Institute of HeartMath, California, 2007

13. <http://www.helpguide.org/mental/adhd_add_signs_symptoms.htm>

14. Midgely, Carol, 'Young and Desperate', *The Times,* London, 26 June 2007

15. ibid.

16. ibid.

17. McCraty, Rollin, Mike Atkinson and Dana Tomasino, *Science of the Heart: Exploring the role of the heart in human performance,* Institute of HeartMath, California, 2007

18. Midgely, Carol, 'Young and Desperate', *The Times,* London, 26 June 2007

19. Norton, Amy, 'Stress Response Tied to Kids' Behavior Problems', *Reuters Health,* 2007, <www.reuters.com/article/healthNews/>

20. Kain, Erik, 'The Finland Phenomenon: Inside the world's most surprising school system', *Forbes,* 2 May 2011

21. Sacks, Oliver, *Musicophilia,* Alfred A. Knopf, New York, 2007

22. Robinson, Sir Ken, 'Schools Kill Creativity', TED, 2006, <http://www.ted. com/talks/ken_robinson_says_schools_kill_creativity.html>

23. Strauss, V., 'Schools Waking Up to Teens' Sleep Needs', *Washington Post*, 10 January 2006

24. Bronson, Po and Ashley Merryman, *NurtureShock*, Hachette Book Group, New York, 2009

25. ibid.

26. Smith, L., *World Socialist Website*, 2004, accessed 11 July 2011, <http://www.wsws.org/index.shtl>

27. Gillian, James, 'Reflections from a Life Behind Bars: Build colleges, not prisons', *Chronicle of Higher Education*, 16 October 1998

28. Robinson, Sir Ken, 'Schools Kill Creativity', TED, 2006, <http://www.ted. com/talks/ken_robinson_says_schools_kill_creativity.html>

29. Murray, J. P., 'The Violent Face of Television: 50 years of research and controversy', in E. L. Palmer and B. M. Young (eds), *The Faces of Televisual Media: Teaching, violence, selling to children*, Mahwa, New Jersey, 2003

30. Gopnik, Blake, '"Batman" Taught Accused Colorado Shooter James Holmes How to Be Crazy', *The Daily Beast*, 25 July 2012, <http://www. thedailybeast.com/articles/2012/07/25/batman-taught-accused-colorado-shooter-james-holmes-how-to-be-crazy.html>

31. Burke, Mary G., 'The Impact of Screen Media on Children', *Environmental Health Perspective*, 18 October 2010

32. Dworak M, T. Schierl, T. Bruns and H. K. Strüder, *Impact of Singular Excessive Computer Game and Television Exposure on Sleep Patterns and Memory Performance of School-aged Children*, Institute of Motor Control and Movement Technique, German Sport University Cologne, <http://www.ncbi.nlm.nih.gov/pubmed/17974734>

33. Murray, J. P., 'The Violent Face of Television: 50 years of research and controversy', in E. L. Palmer and B. M. Young (eds), *The Faces of Televisual Media: Teaching, violence, selling to children*, Mahwa, New Jersey, 2003

34. ibid.

35. ibid.

36. Weir, S. B., '10 Things you Don't Know About Teens and Social Networking', 2011, accessed 26 August 2011, <http://shine.yahoo.com/channel/parenting>

37. Robinson, Sir Ken, 'Schools Kill Creativity', TED, 2006, <http://www.ted.com/talks/ken_robinson_says_schools_kill_creativity.html>

38. Bronson, Po and Ashley Merryman, *NurtureShock*, Hachette Book Group, New York, 2009

39. Garb, David, interview, June 2012

40. ibid.

41. Welsh, Jennifer, 'Stress is More Stressful for Teens', *Livescience*, 21 June 2011, <http://www.livescience.com/14698-teen-stress-brain-nsf-sciencenation.html>

42. ibid.

43. McCraty, Rollin, Mike Atkinson and Dana Tomasino, *Science of the Heart: Exploring the role of the heart in human performance,* Institute of HeartMath, California, 2007

44. ibid.

45. Freely adapted from the Institute of HeartMath's 'Heart Lock-in' technique, <http://www.heartmath.org>

46. McCraty, Rollin, Mike Atkinson, Dana Tomasino and Raymond Trevor Bradley, *The Coherent Heart: Heart–brain neurological interactions, cognitive performance, and the emergence of system-wide order,* Institute of HeartMath, California, 2004

47. Sacks, Oliver, *Musicophilia,* Alfred A. Knopf, New York, 2007

48. The Song Room Research, <http://songroom.org.au/research/the-song-room-research>

49. ibid.

Part Three: Restorative Parenting

1. Grille, Robin, *Parenting for a Peaceful World*, Longueville Media, Sydney, 2005

2. Thorsborne, M., 'Parenting for a Peaceful Home' workshop, interviewed by S. Davidow, Noosa, Australia, July 2011

3. Kohn, Alfie, *Beyond Discipline: From compliance to community*, Association for Supervision & Curriculum Development; 10th Anniversary edition, August 2006

4. ibid.

5. Zehr, Howard, *The Little Book of Restorative Justice*, Good Books, Intercourse, PA, US, 2002

6. Thorsborne, M., 'Parenting for a Peaceful Home' workshop, interviewed by S. Davidow, Noosa, Australia, July 2011

7. Freely adapted from *Seven Essential Aspects of Restorative Parenting*, Colorado Center for Restorative Practices, 2009, <http://www.openpathtrainings.com/boulder-parenting-class>

8. Adapted from McCold, Paul and Wachtel, Ted, 'Figure 1. Social Discipline Window', *From Restorative Justice to Restorative Practices: Expanding the paradigm*, 2000, <http://www.iirp.edu/article_detail.php?article_id=Mzk5>

9. Adapted from Wachtel, Ted, 'Restorative Justice in Everyday Life: Beyond the formal ritual', paper presented at the Reshaping Australian Institutions Conference: Restorative Justice and Civil Society, The Australian National University, Canberra, 16–18 February 1999

ADDITIONAL REFERENCES

Appelhans, Bradley M. and Linda J. Luecken, 'Heart Rate Variability as an Index of Regulated Emotional Responding', *Review of General Psychology,* 2006, vol. 10, no. 3, pp. 229–40

Children's Health and the Environment, <www.who.int/ceh>

Cookson, Bernard Nesfield, *Rudolf Steiner's Vision of Love,* Rudolf Steiner Press, London, 1999

Darragh, O., 'Naplan Nightmares', *Education Review,* 2011

Dweck, C. S., *Self-Theories,* New York, Psychology Press, 2000

Garratt, Peter, '"They're Worth It": Arts curriculum can boost student school experience', Minister for School Education, Early Childhood and Youth Media Release, 22 March 2011

Gray, Chris, 'Stress of early GCSE exams drives schoolgirl, 15, to take her own life', *Independent,* 27 May 2004, retrieved from <http://www.independent.co.uk/news/education/education-news/stress-of-early-gcse-exams-drives-schoolgirl-15-to-take-her-own-life-564897.html>

Immordino-Yang, Mary Helen and Antonio Damasio, 'We Feel, Therefore We Learn: The relevance of affective and social neuroscience to education', *Mind, Brain and Education,* 2007, vol. 1, no.1

McCraty, Rollin, *The Energetic Heart,* Institute of Heartmath, California, 2003

Melcer, Donald, *Self-Development Through Meditative Practice,* St. George Publications, California, 1983

Morris Jr., John A., Patrick R. Norris, Lemuel R. Waitman, Asli Ozdas, Oscar D. Guillamondegui and Judith M. Jenkins, *Adrenal Insufficiency, Heart Rate Variability, and Complex Biologic Systems: A Study of 1,871 Critically Ill Trauma Patients,* Elsevier Inc., New York, 2007

Pfeiffer, Ehernfried, *Heart Lectures,* Mercury Press, New York, 1982

Porges, Stephen W., 'Orienting in a Defensive World: Mammalian modifications of our evolutionary heritage. A Polyvagal Theory', *Psychophysiology*, Cambridge University Press, 1995, vol. 32, pp. 301–18

Segerstrom, Suzanne C. and Lise Solberg Nes, 'Heart Rate Variability Reflects Self-Regulatory Strength, Effort, and Fatigue', *Association for Psychological Science*, University of Kentucky Press, 2007, vol. 18, no. 3

Wilbum, V. R., and D. E. Smith, 'Stress, Self-Esteem and Suicidal Ideation in Late Adolescence', *Adolescence*, 2005, vol. 40, p. 157

Index

A

abandonment 156
abstractions, brain development 123
academic assessment
    FCATs 60–1
    NAPLAN 4–5, 150
    negative effect of 78
    unsound basis 62
    see also formal testing
academic excellence, music students 149
academic failure, risk-taking behaviour 92
academic results, learning environment 68
academic success, suicide attempts 91–2
accelerated learning programs 134
accidents, car 79, 204–5
accountability
    repair process 196
    restorative parenting 167–8
ADD/ADHD, signs and symptoms 65
ADHD
    Australian experience 65
    low HRV 58
    possible cause 45
    response to outdoors 66–7
    school environment 59, 63, 65–7
adrenaline, effect of excess 13
adult conversation 124
adventure, teens' need for 82–4
affirmative statements, ratio of 159
ambiguity, accepting 196
amygdala 89
anti-depressants
    exam pressure 6
    UK child usage 70
appreciation, heart rate 23
architects, government 105
arguments, in front of children 126
arts education
    arts-based programs 149–50
    benefits of 86
    importance to health 68
assignments 75
Australia
    ADHD experience 65
    NAPLAN testing program 4–5, 150
    pathways to university 76
authoritarian parents 167–8
autonomic nervous system 11–13, 20–1
awareness, fostering 195

B

babies
    crying 170–1
    hearing range 30–1
    left to cry 29–30, 37–8
    post-womb environment 28–9
    reaction to noise 30–2
balance, in educational program 68
beach walk 66–7
bedtime, stress-free approach 177–8
biofeedback, technologies enabling 145–6
boredom, teens 83
brain
    glucose metabolism 109
    teens' maturity 199
    teens' pruning phase 142, 198
brain development
    creative activities 86
    dealing with abstractions 123
    linked to the heart 43
    loving contact benefit 45
    school-age children 64
    from seven to fourteen 126
    sleep deprivation 87–9
    teens 131–2, 142
    toddlers 124
breathing
    activities that regulate 140
    heart rate variability 20–1
    regulating 147
    rythmical pattern 147
breaths, daily statistics 81
Bronson, Po 53, 88–9
brown snake bites 10
bullies 193–6
Burke, Dr Mary 109

C
cancer 62–3
car accidents 79, 204–5
cardiovascular disease see heart disease
Carskadon, Mary A. 88
'Child Poverty in Perspective' (UNESCO
  Report) 7
China, student stress 5
climbing on furniture 50
cognitions
  vs emotions 18
  function and development 40
cognitive capacity 22–4
computer games
  effect on children 107
  effect on nervous system 112
  glucose metabolism 109
  the reality of virtual 111–12
  sleep pattern changes 110–11
  stress hormones 112–13
Conner, Michael 71–2
consistency, in parenting 125
'controlled crying' 29–30
cortisol levels, crying babies 30
creativity 84–7
crying, babies 29–30, 37–8, 170–1
cyber-world, instant stress machine 112

D
day care
  differences between centres 34–6
  effect on child 35
  ideal environment 102–3
Dent, Maggie 4
depression
  causes for teens 71–2
  earlier environments 72
  sleep deprivation 89
  UK teens 70–2
development stages
  birth to three 36–8
  changing needs 27–9
  early childhood 49–51
  starting school 63
  understanding 54

see also emotional environment; teens
dinner table, stress at 178
discipline
  restorative 158–9
  retributive 157
  see also punishment
disconnection
  from all media 117–18
  by media 71
  teen years 83
distractions, while shopping 180–1

E
early childhood education
  Finland 77–8
  learning by experiment 49–51
Eastern Oregon Correctional Institute 97–9
eating, stress-free approach 178–80
education, current crisis 77
educational environment
  ADHD 59, 63, 65–7
  aesthetically pleasing 104
  in America 59–61, 136–8
  beneficial 58–9
  conformist 63
  formal testing 78
  high schools 140–2
  physical 56
  preschool 133–4
  pressure for conformity 100–1
  primary schools 135–40
  prison-like 100–2
  school start times 88–90
  students' needs met 104
emotional environment
  from birth to six 119–24
  from fifteen to adult 127
  from seven to fourteen 125–6
emotional state, positive 21–2
emotions
  vs cognitions 18
  effect of 18–19
  parents modelling 122
empathy
  modelled by parents 122–3

need to learn 195
EmWave biofeedback 145–6
enrichment programs 61–2
exams
    anti-depressant use 6
    fear of failure 76–7
    frinal 75–6
    GCSE 5–6
exercise, rhythmical 147
exhalation 82
expectations
    giving children 159
    of mistake-makers 161
    of parents 159–60
    parents of 4-year-olds 160
exploration
    allowing 49
    by toddlers 175
Eysenck, Dr Hans 62

F
Facebook 117
families, functional 79–80
family activities 140
family conferences 200–3
FCATs (Florida Comprehensive
    Assessment Tests) 60–1
fear of flying 84
fight-or-flight response 11–12
'Finish Line Syndrome' 129
Finland, education system 77–8, 139
Florida Comprehensive Assessment Tests
    (FCATs) 60–1
fMRIs
    computer games vs adding numbers 111
    screen media usage 109
    violence on TV 113
foetus
    developmental needs 26–7
    exposure to noises 31
food
    not used as a threat 179–80
    telling story of origin 179
friends, teens need for 80–1
frustration, heart rate 23

functional families 79–80
functional Magnetic Resonance Imaging
    see fMRIs

G
Galvan, Adriana 131
Garrett, Peter 150
GCSE exams 5–6
gifted children 53–4
gifted program
    declined 136
    parent to monitor 138
gratitude 147
guilt 195

H
happiness 51–2
Harlow, Harry 33–4
Harnessing and Directing Energy trick
    50–1
Hart, Daniel 74–5
head-heart entrainment
    children's brainwaves 112
    explained 39–40
    parent and child 46
hearing range, babies 30–1
heart
    electromagnetic field 43–5
    link to brain development 43
    as a sense organ 17–18
heart disease
    price for 24/7 existence 7
    statistics 1
    stress predictive of 63
heart energy exchange 141–2
heart rate variability (HRV)
    explained 20–3
    in newborns 58
heart rhythm patterns
    academic ability 58
    baby-mother entrainment 45
    change responding to environment 56
    computer games, TV 112
    EmWave biofeedback 145
    ordered 39

positive emotional states 21
   while singing 148
high coherence
   achieving 146–7
   heart rhythms 22–3
   state of 43–4
   while singing 148
high schools
   evaluating environment 140–2
   good environment 104
   ugly environment 103–4
hippocampus 89
homework
   solution to refusal of 92–6
   student's view of 75
hot elements, preventing touching 121

I

imagination 84–5
infanticide 156
Institute of HeartMath (IHM) 17–18
intellectual development
   effect of environment 62
   effect of formal testing 78

J

Jakob
   engaged outside the classroom 66–7
   playground accident 189–91
jogging 147

K

kindergarten
   educational environment 133–4
   military environment 101
   noise and busyness levels 59–60
kindness, origins of 121–3

L

learning disabilities 63
lecturing 195
Leeuwkop Prison, South Africa 98
'Lost Hour' of sleep 89

M

make-or-break moment, final exams 75–6
Maushart, Susan 117
meals, stress-free approach 178–80
'Mean World Syndrome' 113
media consumption, influence 111
melatonin secretion 88
meltdowns *see also* tantrums
   managing 173, 182
   physiological effects 47–8
   public 46–8
memory consolidation, during sleep 88,
   109
Merryman, Ashley 53, 88–9
Middle East, life in 120
middle schools, environment 103–4
Middlemiss, Wendy 30
Midgley, Carol 70
mindfulness 144–5
mistakes, allowing children to make 120–2
monkey experiment 33–4
movies 85
music
   antedote for stress 148–51
   boosts teens' energy 86
   soul food 85
Music Excellence program 149
myelin 64

N

name-calling 193–5
NAPLAN (National Assessment Program
   — Literacy and Numeracy 4–5, 150
negative stimuli 89
neglectful parents 167–8
neonatal intensive care units (NICUs) 34–5
nervous system
   autonomic 11–13, 20–1
   effect of computer games 112
   parasympathetic 11–13, 20–1
   sympathetic nervous system 11, 113
neural networks
   myelin sheathed 57
   teens' pruning process 198
neural patterning 22

neurocardiology 18
neurons, sleep deprivation 88
'no,' children saying 177
noise, sensitivity to 30–2
nose, pinched by baby 122
nursing mothers, baby's brainwaves 42
NurtureShock (book) 53, 88–9

O

over-intellectualising 123
oxytocin 17–18

P

parasympathetic nervous system 11–13,
    20–1
parenting
    agreed goals 125–6
    consistency in 125
    low-stress 195–6
    role change with teens 199–200
    styles 49, 167–8, 177
    see also restorative parenting
parents
    asking for feedback 130
    emotional state of 40
    reacting to tantrums 174–7
    reactions to dramas 79
permissive parenting 49, 167–8, 177
phone bill, paid back 161
physiological coherence, heart energy
    exchange 141–2
physiological milestones, in child's
    development 57
playground accidents, restorative approach
    189–91
post-traumatic stress disorder (PTSD)
    brain activity 113–14
    violence on TV 111
prefrontal cortex
    birth to three 36, 74
    dorsolateral 199
    sleep deprivation 88
    teen years 74
    teens' brains 131–2
pregnancy, effects of stress 27

preschoolers
    academic skills 134
    positive environment 134
preschools see kindergarten
Pribram, Dr Karl 73
primary schools
    desired attributes 139–40
    finding best fit 135–6
    Florida US example 136–8
    ideal environment 103
    neural development 138–40
    non-academic program days 61–2
    supportive environment 135–40
    typical day 67–8
prison environment 97–100
private school fees 129–30
PTSD see post-traumatic stress disorder
    (PTSD)
punishment
    price of 158–9
    retributive 157–9
    and reward system 60, 63
    sibling conflicts 183–4
punitive parents 167–8
puppy, dropped in toilet 122

Q

questions
    about the sun 123, 126
    before enrolling child 102–3
    'why' 123
    for Year 9 students 52
quinoa, son eating 179

R

reasons, giving children 159
recidivism prevention 99
recreation 81–2
restorative chats
    bullying incidents 193–5
    disruptive classroom 210
    example 162
    smoking at a party 204
    uses of 161
restorative discipline 158–9

restorative parenting
  explained 155–6, 167–9
  philosophy 164
  sibling conflicts 184–7
  workshop responses 156–7, 163
Restorative Practice 83, 104–5, 155
reward system 60, 63
rhythmical exercise 147
rhythms of life 81–2
risk-taking behaviour 131–2
Robinson, Sir Ken 87, 120
rock throwing 50–1
Rowling, J.K. 85

S
Sacks, Oliver 85, 148
Sapolsky, Robert 12
Sarasota, Florida
  elementary school 59–60
  high school 103
school environment see educational
  environment
school fees, payback promise 129–30
school hours 88–90
scolding 195
Scotland, testing students 4
screaming at children, time for 181–2
screen time
  excessive 110
  family agreement 201
  limiting 117
  violence and neural patterning 107–9
sexual relationships, premature 74
shave horse 145–6
shopping
  coping with 46–8, 174
  distractions during 180–1
shutting-yourself-in-a-room trick 48,
  173–4
sibling conflicts
  preschoolers 183–4
  primary school age 184–7
siblings, unequal freedoms 209
sighing 82
singing, high coherence 148

skateboard ramp 94–5
sleep
  computer games and 110–11
  'Lost Hour' 89
  memory consolidation 88, 109
  slow-wave sleep (SWS) 109–10
sleep deprivation 87–90
sleeping arrangements, with newborns
  37–8
smoking 204–7
social media 71
social networking 114–18
South Africa, after apartheid 155
spanking 121
starting school 63
stone throwing 50–1
stress
  Chinese students 5
  chronic long-term 12–13
  chronic unmanaged 62–3
  at dinner table 178
  explained 10–14
  heart disease link 1–2
  high school workload 75
  long-term impact 7–8
  music as antedote 148–51
  NAPLAN tests 4–5, 150
  physiological changes 72
  rise in children 1
  at school 3–6, 75, 92
  social networking 114–18
  UK students 5–6
stress hormones
  computer games 112–13
  effect of excess 12
  effect on foetus 15–16, 27
  excess adrenaline 13
stress responses
  blueprint formed 73
  greater than usual 74–5
  learned 15–16
  from nurturing environment 72
  'unwriting' 73
stressors, 'buffers' against 73

'success' 51–2, 54
suicide
    academic success link 91–2
    rates 91
    teens 6–7, 76
sun question 123, 126
sympathetic nervous system
    overactive 113
    role of 11

T
tantrums
    helpful action 173
    physiological effects 47–8
    public 46–8
    reacting to 172–3
    responding in kind 174–5
    in waiting room 175–7
    see also meltdowns
teachers, effect on children 56–7
technology, disconnecting from 117–18
teens
    behaviour management 200
    brain pruning phase 142, 198
    depression 70–2
    lacking wisdom 130–1
    misunderstood 127
    need for adventure 82–4
    relationships with parents 127–30
    requests vs commands 129
    risk-taking behaviour 131–2
    in school selection 141
    school workload 75
    sleep deprivation 87–90
    stressed by parents 80
    suicide 6–7, 91–2
    in the UK 70
    value of friends 80–1
    view of the world 71–2
television, violence on 108–9, 111, 113–14
temper tantrums see tantrums
TestEdge program 146
testing in schools see academic assessment;
    exams
The Song Room programs 149–51

The Winter of Our Disconnect (book) 117
Thorsborne, Margaret 155–6
threats, perception of 12–13
toddlers, needs and behaviour 175
touch
    emotional health 73–4
    loving 33–5
    negative perception of 57–8
    in schools 57
'toughen up,' failure to 3
toys, fights over 121
Truth and Reconciliation Commission 155

U
UK, student stress 5–6
university, pathways to 76

V
vandalism 208
vegetables, involvement in growing 178–9
violence
    desensitisation to 113
    on television 108–9, 111
    on TV 113–14
virtual reality, becoming reality 111–12

W
'why' questions 123
Why Zebras Don't Get Ulcers (book) 12
work ethic 95

Y
yelling
    parents 173
    time for 181–2

Also by Exisle Publishing ...

Nurturing a Healthy Mind

Doing what matters most for your child's developing brain

Michael C. Nagel PhD

If you've ever wondered whether enrolling your three-year-old in 'enrichment programs' will give them a head start in life, or have simply despaired at your four-year-old's inability to sit still, you'll find *Nurturing a Healthy Mind* essential reading!

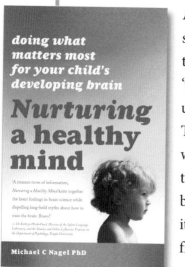

Author Mike Nagel takes the available science on how the brain responds to the environment, processes stimuli and 'thinks', and presents it in an easy-to-understand and user-friendly format. The result is a book that 'translates' what neuroscience is telling us about the development of a child's mind from birth to pre-pubescence. Specifically, it details the development of the brain from infancy to the early school years and explains how this knowledge can help us deal with the everyday realities of raising healthy and happy children.

ISBN 978 1 921966 02 6

Best Start

Understanding your baby's emotional needs to create the best beginnings

Lynn Jenkins BA (Hons), MPsych (Clin)

Your baby's early experiences and interactions provide them with the beginnings of their self-beliefs, thoughts and feelings; their self-esteem and self-value; how they operate in relationships; how they behave socially; and their sense of emotional security. It is therefore vital that you understand how to help your baby to develop trust and confidence, and to feel secure and valued.

In *Best Start*, psychologist Lynn Jenkins looks at how a person's emotional foundations are formed in babyhood and the power that these foundations have over the way in which a child develops. Most importantly, she outlines what your baby needs in order to develop a positive idea of themselves and what you can do to meet those needs, ensuring that your child experiences the best start in life.

ISBN 978 1 921497 89 6